GAMAL ABDEL NASSER

GAMAL ABDEL NASSER

John DeChancie

CHELSEA HOUSE PUBLISHERS
NEW YORK
NEW HAVEN   PHILADELPHIA

EDITOR-IN-CHIEF: Nancy Toff
EXECUTIVE EDITOR: Remmel T. Nunn
MANAGING EDITOR: Karyn Gullen Browne
COPY CHIEF: Juliann Barbato
PICTURE EDITOR: Adrian G. Allen
ART DIRECTOR: Giannella Garrett
MANUFACTURING MANAGER: Gerald Levine

Staff for GAMAL ABDEL NASSER:

SENIOR EDITOR: John W. Selfridge
ASSISTANT EDITORS: Pierre Hauser, Kathleen McDermott, Bert Yaeger
EDITORIAL ASSISTANT: James Guiry
COPY EDITORS: Gillian Bucky, Sean Dolan, Michael Goodman, Ellen Scordato
ASSISTANT PICTURE EDITOR: Juliette Dickstein
SENIOR DESIGNER: David Murray
ASSISTANT DESIGNER: Jill Goldreyer
DESIGNERS: Laura Lang, Donna Sinisgalli
PICTURE RESEARCH: Cheryl Moch
PRODUCTION COORDINATOR: Laura McCormick
COVER ILLUSTRATION: Michael Garland

CREATIVE DIRECTOR: Harold Steinberg

Frontispiece courtesy of UPI/Bettmann

3   5   7   9   8   6   4   2

Library of Congress Cataloging in Publication Data

DeChancie, John. GAMAL ABDEL NASSER

(World leaders past & present)
Bibliography: p.
Includes index.
1. Nasser, Gamal Abdel, 1918–1970—Juvenile literature.
2. Egypt—Presidents—Biography—Juvenile literature.
[1. Nasser, Gamal Abdel, 1918–1970. 2. Egypt—
Presidents] I. Title. II. Series
DT107.83.D42   1988   962'.053'0924 [B] [92]   87-15065

ISBN 0-87754-542-1

Contents

ADENAUER
ALEXANDER THE GREAT
MARC ANTONY
KING ARTHUR
ATATÜRK
ATTLEE
BEGIN
BEN-GURION
BISMARCK
LÉON BLUM
BOLÍVAR
CESARE BORGIA
BRANDT
BREZHNEV
CAESAR
CALVIN
CASTRO
CATHERINE THE GREAT
CHARLEMAGNE
CHIANG KAI-SHEK
CHURCHILL
CLEMENCEAU
CLEOPATRA
CORTÉS
CROMWELL
DANTON
DE GAULLE
DE VALERA
DISRAELI
EISENHOWER
ELEANOR OF AQUITAINE
QUEEN ELIZABETH I
FERDINAND AND ISABELLA
FRANCO

FREDERICK THE GREAT
INDIRA GANDHI
MOHANDAS GANDHI
GARIBALDI
GENGHIS KHAN
GLADSTONE
GORBACHEV
HAMMARSKJÖLD
HENRY VIII
HENRY OF NAVARRE
HINDENBURG
HITLER
HO CHI MINH
HUSSEIN
IVAN THE TERRIBLE
ANDREW JACKSON
JEFFERSON
JOAN OF ARC
POPE JOHN XXIII
LYNDON JOHNSON
JUÁREZ
JOHN F. KENNEDY
KENYATTA
KHOMEINI
KHRUSHCHEV
MARTIN LUTHER KING, JR.
KISSINGER
LENIN
LINCOLN
LLOYD GEORGE
LOUIS XIV
LUTHER
JUDAS MACCABEUS
MAO ZEDONG

MARY, QUEEN OF SCOTS
GOLDA MEIR
METTERNICH
MUSSOLINI
NAPOLEON
NASSER
NEHRU
NERO
NICHOLAS II
NIXON
NKRUMAH
PERICLES
PERÓN
QADDAFI
ROBESPIERRE
ELEANOR ROOSEVELT
FRANKLIN D. ROOSEVELT
THEODORE ROOSEVELT
SADAT
STALIN
SUN YAT-SEN
TAMERLANE
THATCHER
TITO
TROTSKY
TRUDEAU
TRUMAN
VICTORIA
WASHINGTON
WEIZMANN
WOODROW WILSON
XERXES
ZHOU ENLAI

ON LEADERSHIP
Arthur M. Schlesinger, jr.

LEADERSHIP, it may be said, is really what makes the world go round. Love no doubt smooths the passage; but love is a private transaction between consenting adults. Leadership is a public transaction with history. The idea of leadership affirms the capacity of individuals to move, inspire, and mobilize masses of people so that they act together in pursuit of an end. Sometimes leadership serves good purposes, sometimes bad; but whether the end is benign or evil, great leaders are those men and women who leave their personal stamp on history.

Now, the very concept of leadership implies the proposition that individuals can make a difference. This proposition has never been universally accepted. From classical times to the present day, eminent thinkers have regarded individuals as no more than the agents and pawns of larger forces, whether the gods and goddesses of the ancient world or, in the modern era, race, class, nation, the dialectic, the will of the people, the spirit of the times, history itself. Against such forces, the individual dwindles into insignificance.

So contends the thesis of historical determinism. Tolstoy's great novel *War and Peace* offers a famous statement of the case. Why, Tolstoy asked, did millions of men in the Napoleonic wars, denying their human feelings and their common sense, move back and forth across Europe slaughtering their fellows? "The war," Tolstoy answered, "was bound to happen simply because it was bound to happen." All prior history predetermined it. As for leaders, they, Tolstoy said, "are but the labels that serve to give a name to an end and, like labels, they have the least possible connection with the event." The greater the leader, "the more conspicuous the inevitability and the predestination of every act he commits." The leader, said Tolstoy, is "the slave of history."

Determinism takes many forms. Marxism is the determinism of class. Nazism the determinism of race. But the idea of men and women as the slaves of history runs athwart the deepest human instincts. Rigid determinism abolishes the idea of human freedom—

the assumption of free choice that underlies every move we make, every word we speak, every thought we think. It abolishes the idea of human responsibility, since it is manifestly unfair to reward or punish people for actions that are by definition beyond their control. No one can live consistently by any deterministic creed. The Marxist states prove this themselves by their extreme susceptibility to the cult of leadership.

More than that, history refutes the idea that individuals make no difference. In December 1931 a British politician crossing Park Avenue in New York City between 76th and 77th Streets around 10:30 P.M. looked in the wrong direction and was knocked down by an automobile—a moment, he later recalled, of a man aghast, a world aglare: "I do not understand why I was not broken like an eggshell or squashed like a gooseberry." Fourteen months later an American politician, sitting in an open car in Miami, Florida, was fired on by an assassin; the man beside him was hit. Those who believe that individuals make no difference to history might well ponder whether the next two decades would have been the same had Mario Constasino's car killed Winston Churchill in 1931 and Giuseppe Zangara's bullet killed Franklin Roosevelt in 1933. Suppose, in addition, that Adolf Hitler had been killed in the street fighting during the Munich *Putsch* of 1923 and that Lenin had died of typhus during World War I. What would the 20th century be like now?

For better or for worse, individuals do make a difference. "The notion that a people can run itself and its affairs anonymously," wrote the philosopher William James, "is now well known to be the silliest of absurdities. Mankind does nothing save through initiatives on the part of inventors, great or small, and imitation by the rest of us—these are the sole factors in human progress. Individuals of genius show the way, and set the patterns, which common people then adopt and follow."

Leadership, James suggests, means leadership in thought as well as in action. In the long run, leaders in thought may well make the greater difference to the world. But, as Woodrow Wilson once said, "Those only are leaders of men, in the general eye, who lead in action. . . . It is at their hands that new thought gets its translation into the crude language of deeds." Leaders in thought often invent in solitude and obscurity, leaving to later generations the tasks of imitation. Leaders in action—the leaders portrayed in this series—have to be effective in their own time.

And they cannot be effective by themselves. They must act in response to the rhythms of their age. Their genius must be adapted, in a phrase of William James's, "to the receptivities of the moment." Leaders are useless without followers. "There goes the mob," said the French politician hearing a clamor in the streets. "I am their leader. I must follow them." Great leaders turn the inchoate emotions of the mob to purposes of their own. They seize on the opportunities of their time, the hopes, fears, frustrations, crises, potentialities. They succeed when events have prepared the way for them, when the community is awaiting to be aroused, when they can provide the clarifying and organizing ideas. Leadership ignites the circuit between the individual and the mass and thereby alters history.

It may alter history for better or for worse. Leaders have been responsible for the most extravagant follies and most monstrous crimes that have beset suffering humanity. They have also been vital in such gains as humanity has made in individual freedom, religious and racial tolerance, social justice and respect for human rights.

There is no sure way to tell in advance who is going to lead for good and who for evil. But a glance at the gallery of men and women in *World Leaders—Past and Present* suggests some useful tests.

One test is this: do leaders lead by force or by persuasion? By command or by consent? Through most of history leadership was exercised by the divine right of authority. The duty of followers was to defer and to obey. "Theirs not to reason why,/ Theirs but to do and die." On occasion, as with the so-called "enlightened despots" of the 18th century in Europe, absolutist leadership was animated by humane purposes. More often, absolutism nourished the passion for domination, land, gold and conquest and resulted in tyranny.

The great revolution of modern times has been the revolution of equality. The idea that all people should be equal in their legal condition has undermined the old structure of authority, hierarchy and deference. The revolution of equality has had two contrary effects on the nature of leadership. For equality, as Alexis de Tocqueville pointed out in his great study *Democracy in America*, might mean equality in servitude as well as equality in freedom.

"I know of only two methods of establishing equality in the political world," Tocqueville wrote. "Rights must be given to every citizen, or none at all to anyone . . . save one, who is the master of all." There was no middle ground "between the sovereignty of all and the absolute power of one man." In his astonishing prediction of 20th-century totalitarian dictatorship, Tocqueville explained how the revolution of equality could lead to the *"Führerprinzip"* and more terrible absolutism than the world had ever known.

But when rights are given to every citizen and the sovereignty of all is established, the problem of leadership takes a new form, becomes more exacting than ever before. It is easy to issue commands and enforce them by the rope and the stake, the concentration camp and the *gulag.* It is much harder to use argument and achievement to overcome opposition and win consent. The Founding Fathers of the United States understood the difficulty. They believed that history had given them the opportunity to decide, as Alexander Hamilton wrote in the first Federalist Paper, whether men are indeed capable of basing government on "reflection and choice, or whether they are forever destined to depend . . . on accident and force."

Government by reflection and choice called for a new style of leadership and a new quality of followership. It required leaders to be responsive to popular concerns, and it required followers to be active and informed participants in the process. Democracy does not eliminate emotion from politics; sometimes it fosters demagoguery; but it is confident that, as the greatest of democratic leaders put it, you cannot fool all of the people all of the time. It measures leadership by results and retires those who overreach or falter or fail.

It is true that in the long run despots are measured by results too. But they can postpone the day of judgment, sometimes indefinitely, and in the meantime they can do infinite harm. It is also true that democracy is no guarantee of virtue and intelligence in government, for the voice of the people is not necessarily the voice of God. But democracy, by assuring the right of opposition, offers built-in resistance to the evils inherent in absolutism. As the theologian Reinhold Niebuhr summed it up, "Man's capacity for justice makes democracy possible, but man's inclination to injustice makes democracy necessary."

A second test for leadership is the end for which power is sought. When leaders have as their goal the supremacy of a master race or the promotion of totalitarian revolution or the acquisition and exploitation of colonies or the protection of greed and privilege or the preservation of personal power, it is likely that their leadership will do little to advance the cause of humanity. When their goal is the abolition of slavery, the liberation of women, the enlargement of opportunity for the poor and powerless, the extension of equal rights to racial minorities, the defense of the freedoms of expression and opposition, it is likely that their leadership will increase the sum of human liberty and welfare.

Leaders have done great harm to the world. They have also conferred great benefits. You will find both sorts in this series. Even "good" leaders must be regarded with a certain wariness. Leaders are not demigods; they put on their trousers one leg after another just like ordinary mortals. No leader is infallible, and every leader needs to be reminded of this at regular intervals. Irreverence irritates leaders but is their salvation. Unquestioning submission corrupts leaders and demands followers. Making a cult of a leader is always a mistake. Fortunately hero worship generates its own antidote. "Every hero," said Emerson, "becomes a bore at last."

The signal benefit the great leaders confer is to embolden the rest of us to live according to our own best selves, to be active, insistent, and resolute in affirming our own sense of things. For great leaders attest to the reality of human freedom against the supposed inevitabilities of history. And they attest to the wisdom and power that may lie within the most unlikely of us, which is why Abraham Lincoln remains the supreme example of great leadership. A great leader, said Emerson, exhibits new possibilities to all humanity. "We feed on genius. . . . Great men exist that there may be greater men."

Great leaders, in short, justify themselves by emancipating and empowering their followers. So humanity struggles to master its destiny, remembering with Alexis de Tocqueville: "It is true that around every man a fatal circle is traced beyond which he cannot pass; but within the wide verge of that circle he is powerful and free; as it is with man, so with communities."

1

Egypt: A Land in Bondage

On a cool spring night in Cairo, 1952, several gunmen crouched outside the home of a high-ranking Egyptian army officer. Among them was career officer Lieutenant Colonel Gamal Abdel Nasser. Nasser was a veteran of street demonstrations against the British-backed Egyptian government, but this assassination attempt would be his first real taste of violent revolution.

Out on the road, car headlights approached. With one hand Nasser signaled forward the squad that would actually do the shooting. One of the men looked back at him and nodded acknowledgment. Nasser was struck by the irony of the situation. Though it was the British who had treated Egypt as a colony since late in the previous century, it was an Egyptian general who was their target. Nevertheless, the general was a tool of British imperialism and had to die.

Foreign interventionism was suffered beyond the limits of decency.
—JACQUES BERQUE
French historian

Gamal Abdel Nasser began his career as an officer in the Egyptian army, working to liberate Egypt from British colonial rule. He led the coup that toppled King Farouk in 1952 and became prime minister and then president of Egypt.

Anti-British demonstrators in Cairo in 1951. British influence in Egypt increased steadily throughout the 19th century; Great Britain's invasion in 1882 began a military presence in the country that lasted until 1956.

The young officers waiting in the darkness were members of a group called the Society of Free Officers. First formed during World War II as an opposition group to King Farouk and the British presence in Egypt, the movement gained momentum and added support after Egypt's humiliating defeat by Israel after that nation declared its independence in 1948. Nasser had been planning and organizing well before that time. Shortly after his commission as an army officer in 1938, he began to discuss the need for revolution. None of these early opposition movements within the military were as well organized as the Free Officers, whose discipline enabled them to avoid detection. The Free Officers lacked clearly defined political objectives; their stated enemies were feudalism, monarchy, and imperialism.

The car turned into a driveway and approached the house. The silence of the night seemed to deepen. Nasser held his breath. He could see nothing but headlights and the dark outline of the car against a dimly lit window. He hoped the forward squad could see better than he could.

A volley of shots rang out. The men of the assassination squad ran past on their way to the road. Nasser raised his pistol to cover their retreat, but no answering shots came. A woman screamed, and a small child began to cry. He jumped to his feet and signaled to the other men in the backup squad. They ran to the waiting getaway cars and piled in. The cars sped off, leaving behind pitiable cries of terror.

Nasser did not sleep that night. The anguished cries from the wife and child of the man they had intended to kill haunted him like a nightmare from which there was no waking. Had Nasser and his men slaughtered an entire family? He wondered how he would ever live with himself if that had happened. He even found himself hoping that their intended target, the general, had survived the attack.

When the next morning's newspaper arrived, Nasser frantically read the story of the assassination attempt. It was with immense relief that he learned that the general had sustained serious wounds but would live and that his family had not been hurt.

Nasser was a patriot. He had taken part in the assassination plot for only one reason: to hasten the day of Egypt's liberation. Nasser's long period of opposition to the government and the British had been noteworthy for the patience he displayed. He was convinced that only the army could successfully carry out the revolution, and in contrast with some of his colleagues, notably Anwar Sadat, he generally did not believe terrorism would aid their cause. For 14 years Nasser had waited for the proper time for the revolution. The bungled assassination confirmed his views.

West of the city of Giza, along the Nile River, the pyramids stand as monuments to Egypt's ancient past. With the victory of Napoléon Bonaparte at the Battle of the Pyramids in 1798, the French gained control of Egypt, beginning more than 150 years of European colonial domination.

Cleopatra, shown receiving her lover, the Roman general and politician Marc Antony, was the last Ptolemaic ruler of Egypt. After the defeat of Marc Antony and Cleopatra in 30 B.C. by the Roman leader Octavius (later Augustus), Egypt became a Roman province.

Egypt was no stranger to foreign domination. One of the world's most ancient civilizations, heir to a legacy of technological achievements, architectural wonders, and a rich literary and religious tradition, Egypt had been under the sway of various foreign conquerors since the 6th century B.C.

Egypt is in northeast Africa, bordered on the north by the Mediterranean Sea and on the east by the Red Sea. The history of the nation is largely the history of civilization along the Nile River. The longest river in the world, it flows south to north through the length of the country. Today 99 percent of the Egyptian population lives along its banks.

Egypt's location has made it the crossroads of conquerors throughout history. The reign of the pharaohs, as Egypt's ancient kings were known, ended in 525 B.C. with the Persian invasion. The Persian empire had expanded from what is now Iran to extend from the Nile to the Indus River. After nearly 200 years of Persian rule, Egypt was occupied by Alexander the Great, who had smashed the Persian empire and conquered most of the known world. Alexander was from Macedonia, which had achieved dominance over the rest of Greece, and his occupation of Egypt at the head of a Greek and Macedonian army introduced Greek influence there. After his death in 323 B.C. Egypt was administered by the Greek general Ptolemy. The Ptolemaic dynasty ruled for almost 300 years. Cleopatra was the last Ptolemaic monarch, but by the time of her reign Egypt had become a pawn in power struggles between factions within the Roman empire. After the defeat of the forces of Cleopatra and Marc Antony — her lover and an important Roman politician and general — in 30 B.C. by the Roman Octavius (later Augustus) and their subsequent suicides, Egypt became a Roman province. Under Roman and Greek influence Egypt became a largely Christian country.

Christianity in Egypt was virtually extinguished by a powerful new force that came like a desert wind out of Arabia, transforming everything in its path. The force was Islam, the religion founded by Muhammad, who lived from A.D. 570 to 632 and called himself the "Prophet of Allah" (God). His followers were called Muslims. By the early 8th century Muslim conquests had carried the new religion from its holy city of Mecca on the Arabian Peninsula throughout the Middle East, Asia, North Africa, and into Spain. The Arab invaders reached Egypt in 639, and by 642 they had succeeded in wresting control from Egypt's Byzantine governor. (The Byzantine empire was the eastern successor of Rome; its capital was Constantinople.) Islamic dynasties ruled Egypt for the next nine centuries, until the ascendancy of the Ottoman Turks in the early 15th century. The country became overwhelmingly Muslim. The Ottoman Turks maintained a loose control over Egypt for the next three centuries.

In the 19th century Ottoman influence in Egypt waned as British and French strength there increased. Egypt was particularly important to Britain as it provided an access, via the Red Sea, to its prize colony, India. In 1854 French engineers obtained from Egypt's ruler, Said Pasha, the concession to build the Suez Canal, which would directly link the Mediterranean and Red seas. The canal was to play an important role in subsequent Egyptian history and in the life of Gamal Abdel Nasser. By 1880 the Egyptian government was effectively controlled by Great Britain and France. When a nationalist rebellion occurred in 1882, British troops defeated the rebels and began more than a half-century of military occupation.

The teeming streets of the historic city of Alexandria, where Nasser was born in January 1918.

Gamal Abdel Nasser was born on January 15, 1918, in the ancient city of Alexandria, the first child of Abdel Nasser Hussein, a postal clerk, and Fahima Hammad, the daughter of an Alexandria businessman. (Egyptians traditionally place the given name before their father's given name; few people have family names.) When he was three the family moved to Beni Mor, the peasant village of his father's birth.

Beni Mor left a lasting impression on Nasser. Situated 230 miles south of Cairo, on the banks of the Nile in the area known as Upper Egypt, it was typical of the region's villages, nothing more than a grouping of mud-colored clay huts shaded by the occasional palm tree and surrounded by acres of irrigated farmland. Except for the banks of the Nile, Egypt is desert. There is very little rainfall. Egyptian peasants have lived the same way for thousands of years, dependent on the Nile for its life-giving water. The *fellahin* (peasants), then as now, coaxed a subsistence living out of small plots on which they grew grain, vegetables, and cotton. Irrigation was crucial, and the technology used to run the system of canals and irrigation ditches was extremely primitive. The pharaoh's royal waterworks inspector would have found few surprises in Beni Mor in 1920.

Because Egypt is predominantly desert, the *fellahin* (peasants) must use the Nile to irrigate their land. The waterwheel in this 1924 photograph is similar to the primitive implements used in the village of Beni Mor, where Nasser grew up. Similar irrigation methods had been used since the days of the pharaohs.

Abdel Nasser Hussein was a low-level government employee. His salary was meager, but his family's life was not as bone-grinding and hopeless as that of the average Egyptian citizen. He was able to afford to send his son Gamal to school in the nearby provincial seat of Asyut. Gamal was not a particularly good student. He was somewhat rebellious, as indicated by one story told of his early life: his father had forbidden him to dig in the family garden, but Gamal, undaunted, dug a hole so big that the elder Nasser fell into it.

Abdel Nasser Hussein's civil service career was a series of moves from one post to another. Deciding that such an uprooted existence would not be good for Gamal, in 1925 he sent the boy to live with an uncle in Cairo. Gamal spent only four years in Beni Mor, but he would always refer to the place as his home and would always consider himself of peasant stock. When he later learned something of politics and economics, he would criticize the essentially feudal structure of Egyptian rural life, characterized by an impoverished, essentially landless, agricultural peasantry and an absentee landholding class, as one of the chief causes of poverty and injustice. Land reform and redistribution would one day dominate his thinking on domestic social issues.

Egypt's largest city, Cairo, is overlooked by the walled citadel, dominated by the mosque of Muhammad Ali, regarded as the founder of modern Egypt. Under his rule, from 1811 to 1849, Egypt reorganized its military, government, and educational system along European lines.

The mosque of Muhammad Ali is visible through the gateway to Cairo's Arab quarter. Nasser came to Cairo to stay with his uncle Khalil in 1925; it was Khalil's tales of his revolutionary exploits that first inspired anti-British sentiment in the young boy.

Gamal arrived at his uncle Khalil's house in March 1925. He was seven years old. To the young rural boy Cairo was a different universe. The streets were thick with traffic, and life throbbed everywhere. His new school was in the heart of the commercial district, not far from Al Azhar, the great Islamic university. He liked Cairo and got along with his uncle, who had spent time in prison for organizing anti-British demonstrations and told Gamal tales of revolutionary intrigue, although he missed his mother. Thus it was the greatest of shocks when the young boy returned home after a year's separation and discovered that she had recently died. It is unclear why Gamal was not told of his mother's death when it happened, and he never forgave his father for failing to tell him or for his quick remarriage. His next three years in Cairo were darkened by the shadow of that sad event. His family life, at least in emotional terms, all but ended.

His father was reassigned to a post in Alexandria in 1929 and sent for his son. The boy spent the next four years in the city of his birth, attending the

Egyptian equivalent of junior high school. Once again he was not a good student. He preferred running through the sun-drenched streets with his playmates or going to the cinema. He was especially fond of American films.

In 1933 the family moved to Cairo, and here a change came over the young Nasser. Enrolled in the Al Nahda Al Misria School — the equivalent of high school — he suddenly discovered that learning could be more than just a chore. He began to read on his own. Native writers attracted him most, among them Mustafa Kemal, leader of a 19th-century Egyptian nationalist movement. He liked the homespun poetry of Ahmed Shawki and the rural novels of Tewfik el-Hakim. He also read foreign authors and especially admired Voltaire, the great 18th-century French satirist and philosopher, and Shakespeare, the English dramatist. Shakespeare's play *Julius Caesar* was Nasser's favorite, and he once played the lead in a student production.

Gamal Nasser may have admired English literature, but he had no admiration for the English. In Cairo he was constantly exposed to nationalist and revolutionary thought. He began to view Britain as merely the latest of Egypt's conquerors, a domineering foreign power. For the first time he considered the possibility that something could be done to force foreign powers to leave Egypt. Aware of the rising tide of Egyptian nationalism surging around him, he participated in his first street demonstration and was arrested by the police. He joined the Young Egypt party, a nationalist group modeled on the Fascist party of Italian leader Benito Mussolini. Although Nasser resigned two years later, he quickly found others with whom he could discuss Egypt's future.

British historian George Young has written that "in the Orient [the East], adolescents are more quick to take political action than men." The young Nasser had already determined the path his life would take. Although as he matured his political perceptions would sharpen, he would remain steadfast in his dedication to Egyptian independence and an end to British imperialism.

Today who can stand up, who can fight back? They say the Egyptian is cowardly. . . . He only needs a leader who will lead him into battle. Then this Egyptian will be a thunderbolt which will make the edifice of persecution tremble.
—NASSER

2

War in North Africa

By the 1930s Great Britain had ruled Egypt for decades, exercising a distant but firm control through a line of puppet rulers. These Egyptian rulers were descendants of Muhammad Ali, a Turkish governor who seized power in 1805, rebelled against Ottoman influence, and established a dynasty. His successful military campaigns in the Sudan, the Arabian Peninsula, and Asia Minor brought the intervention of the Ottoman Empire, Great Britain, and France, who combined in 1841 to force him to relinquish much of his gains but confirmed him and his heirs as hereditary rulers of Egypt. After his death in 1849 his descendants were subject to increased British and French interference while still paying nominal allegiance to the Ottomans. It was his son Said Pasha who in 1854 granted the French engineer and diplomat Ferdinand de Lesseps the concession to build the Suez Canal. At first, Egypt retained a major share of control in the canal, but in 1875 Ali's grandson Ismail Pasha sold his country's canal stock to Great Britain to make up a deficit in the royal treasury. Ismail was a weak leader. His

> *To live in despair is not to live at all.*
> —MUSTAFA KAMEL
> Egyptian nationalist
> admired by Nasser

Nasser continued to wear his military uniform even after becoming Egypt's president. He became convinced early in his career as an officer that only the army could successfully carry out a revolution, and he organized the Free Officers to accomplish that goal.

UPI/BETTMANN NEWSPHOTOS

government's bankruptcy further enabled France and Britain to consolidate their hold on Egypt. In 1882 an Egyptian army revolt against Ismail's son Tewfik was put down by British soldiers. Thereafter Great Britain alone ruled Egypt.

Although British control brought an end to some of the worst excesses of Turkish rule, such as the repressive taxation of Ismail's reign, native Egyptians were still second-class citizens in their own country. Foreigners still dominated Egypt. Until the outbreak of World War I and the Ottoman Empire's subsequent defeat, Turkish influence remained strong; Turkish landlords collected rent from Egyptian peasants, and the lower civil service and military still had a large Turkish element. The educated classes were predominantly not Egyptian, and Greek, Italian, and French merchants controlled commerce and industry. Over it all ruled the British civil service and military. For the most part, native Egyptians were consigned to the lower ranks of the economic order; those who were not unemployed were peasants, laborers, and struggling tradesmen.

Egypt in the 1940s was a nation of contrasts — modern and the ancient, rich and poor, rural and the urban, colonial and native — as this 1942 Cairo street scene demonstrates. Establishments like this English billiard room often featured signs stating "No Dogs or Egyptians Allowed."

Egyptian nationalism lay dormant, but every so often it would stir a bit in its long sleep. In 1919 a nationalist political party called *Wafd*, which means "delegation" in Arabic, was formed. By 1923 it had persuaded the British to permit the drafting of a constitution and to allow national elections early the following year. The elections were held, and the nationalists won a majority in the new parliament. A Wafd leader, Saad Zaghlul, was appointed prime minister. For the first time in its long history Egypt had an elected government, but this independence was short-lived. When the British commander of the Egyptian army was murdered in Cairo a few months after the elections, High Commissioner Lord Allenby delivered an ultimatum to the Wafd consisting of a number of demands that would have rendered the government virtually powerless. Particularly galling was the demand that all Egyptian troops be withdrawn from the Sudan, to the south, which Egypt had long considered as its own. Zaghlul resigned rather than submit to humiliation. New elections were held, and a more pro-British party controlled the parliament. When the Wafd won a majority in

Egypt was an important military base of the Allies during World War II. The British were so thoroughly resented that many Egyptians welcomed the possible German invasion as a "liberation."

the elections of 1925, King Fuad (he had received the title when the British formally ended the protectorate they had declared over Egypt from 1914 to 1922) dissolved parliament. It remained dissolved until 1935. The constitution of 1923 granted the king the right to appoint ministers without regard to election results. He could also dissolve parliament at any time. Although the nationalists might get the votes of Egypt's masses, the British and the king could choose to appoint subservient ministers and dissolve parliament. In 1928 the British suspended the entire constitution.

In 1935 a 17-year-old Nasser wrote:

> Egypt is in a state of hopeless despair. . . . Who can cry halt to the imperialists? . . . Where is the man to rebuild the country so that the weak and humiliated Egyptian people can rise again and live as free and independent men? . . . The nation sleeps like men in a cave. Who can waken these miserable creatures who do not even know who they are?

Nasser knew that Egypt would rise to full-fledged nationhood only on the wings of a resurgent national spirit, a spirit that could only come from the awakened Egyptian masses, but he also knew that a small group of leaders — perhaps just one man — was needed to guide and nurture that spirit, to tap its power to achieve the ultimate goal of Egypt's independence. Even at this early stage, he may have envisioned himself as that man.

Public demonstrations were commonplace in Egypt during the 1930s and often turned violent. As a student Nasser participated in many such protests and was once slightly wounded.

By the 1930s the Egyptian nationalist movement had splintered. With the death of Saad Zaghlul the Wafd split into factions, ranging from staunch nationalists to those advocating collaboration with the monarchy. At the same time an extremist Islamic fundamentalist party, the Muslim Brotherhood, grew in power. Founded by Hassan el-Banna in 1928, the Muslim Brotherhood was initially not overtly political, calling for the purging of Western and secular elements from Egyptian society. In the 1930s it began to advocate Egyptian independence and the establishment of an Islamic constitution based on the teachings of the Koran, the sacred text of Islam. By the end of the decade el-Banna had established a secret terrorist wing to achieve the organization's goals. The Brotherhood's militancy, if not its specific program of action, was to influence Nasser in his quest for Egyptian freedom.

By 1935 the Wafd had been out of power for 12 years, and the constitution had been suspended for 7. In November of that year the British foreign secretary gave a speech reiterating his opposition to restoring the constitution and to any change in Egypt's colonial status. Cairo was wracked by demonstrations in response. British soldiers fired on

A 16-year-old King Farouk (center) inspects his honor guard shortly after succeeding his father, Fuad, in 1936. The weakness of the Egyptian monarchy was revealed on February 4, 1942, when British tanks surrounded the royal palace and forced Farouk to appoint a new prime minister.

27

one of these assemblies, killing a student. As president of the High School Students' Association, Nasser organized a march on a British army garrison in Cairo, during the course of which two more students were killed and he was slightly wounded.

Worried by the turmoil, King Fuad, with British approval, restored constitutional rights and called for national elections. The Wafd was promptly voted into power, and Mustafa Nahas, a former associate of Zaghlul, became prime minister. The following year Nahas shocked his supporters by signing a treaty that guaranteed a continued British military presence in Egypt for the next 20 years, though formally changing the terms of the presence from a military occupation to a military alliance and permitting British troops only along the Suez Canal.

Nasser almost despaired. Ironically, the 1936 treaty provided the means for Nasser's own rise to power. Egypt was now required to participate more actively in its military alliance with Britain. To meet the leadership needs of an expanded Egyptian army the Royal Military Academy at Abbassia, on the outskirts of Cairo, began accepting the applications of young men from all classes; previously only the sons of the upper class had been admitted. Though Nasser first tried law school, he grew disillusioned after seven months and quit. The eased restrictions for admission to the military academy provided him with another opportunity. Nasser was aware that the revamped military could prove to be a strong institution within Egypt (at present it was essentially a police force under the control of British officers) and could provide a young firebrand with a strong base from which to undertake his plans for reform. Though initially rejected for admission because of his reputation as an activist and troublemaker, Nasser persisted. He obtained an interview with the undersecretary of state for war and convinced the man to admit him. In March 1937 Nasser took his place at the academy among the first class of "new officers" from the lower classes.

The rapid expansion of the Egyptian army necessitated a greatly accelerated officer training course at the academy. Nasser spent 16 months there, studying military science, mathematics, history, and administration. He also read widely on his own, chiefly history and biographies of such figures as the French Emperor Napoleon Bonaparte and the British leader of the Arab forces in World War I, T. E. Lawrence. He showed evidence of leadership ability and was soon commanding new cadets.

The accelerated course led to a commission in July 1938. Second Lieutenant Nasser's first assignment was an infantry post in Mankabad, in Upper Egypt. There he met fellow officer Anwar Sadat, whose career would intertwine with his. Sadat was also of humble Nile village origins. He and Nasser became fast friends. They and other officers with similar political feelings would spend evenings discussing Egypt's future.

In October 1942 Germany's Afrika Korps, under General Erwin Rommel (center), approached the Nile and threatened Allied control of Egypt and the Suez. The German defeat at the Egyptian town of El Alamein was a turning point in World War II.

UPI/BETTMANN NEWSPHOTOS

Although the Arabs had been willing and valuable soldiers for the British in World War I, particularly under the command of the legendary T. E. Lawrence ("Lawrence of Arabia"), British-trained Arab forces saw little actual combat during World War II.

In 1939 World War II broke out in Europe. France and Great Britain (and later the Soviet Union and the United States) allied against Germany and Italy. In 1941 Japan joined Germany and Italy and fought the Allies in the Pacific. Egypt broke diplomatic relations with Germany but remained officially neutral. By October 1942 German troops under General

Erwin Rommel, called the "Desert Fox," had driven
eastward across North Africa and were within 60
miles of the Nile.

At this precarious point for the British and Allied
effort, Egyptian resentment of the British had
reached a high point. Despite the doctrine of racial
superiority practiced and preached by Germany's

Nazi dictator Adolf Hitler — he had over 6 million Jews, Poles, Ukrainians, gypsies, and other ethnic and national groups put to death in concentration camps during the war — many Egyptians viewed the prospect of a German victory as an opportunity to finally rid themselves of the British. For this same reason, Ireland, which had also suffered under British colonial rule, refused to support Britain during the war, while in India, which was struggling for its independence from the British, some leaders advocated not fighting the Japanese should they invade.

"The enemy of my enemy is my friend" says an Arab proverb, and many Egyptians were willing to take a chance with Hitler's virulent racism if it would free them from the British. Conspiracies existed within the government and the military. Sadat, for example, was involved early in the war in an unsuccessful plot to smuggle the former Egyptian chief of staff, Aziz Misri, who had been dismissed by the British because of his pro-German sympathies, to Rommel.

Aware of the pro-German sentiment, the British had, on February 4, 1942, surrounded the palace of King Farouk and forced him to install the Wafd leader Mustafa Nahas as prime minister. The British felt only the Wafd among Egypt's political parties believed both British and Egyptian interests would be served by an Allied victory and commanded sufficient popular support to govern.

The British action left nationalist Egyptians feeling humiliated. Though the two nations were ostensibly military allies, the British strong-arm tactics seemed to demonstrate more clearly the countries' relationship. Once again the colonial lord had imposed its will upon its dependent servant. The new nationalist officers within Egypt's military were outraged. Then stationed in the Sudan, Nasser declared that he was "ashamed" that the army had not acted against the British. Upon his return to Egypt shortly afterward, he began to organize the group known as the Free Officers. Later, Nasser said that February 4, 1942, was the day his revolution was born.

But the time was not yet right for the Free Officers. In October of 1942 British forces under General Bernard Montgomery defeated Rommel's *Afrika Korps* in a battle near the western Egyptian desert town of El Alamein. El Alamein was a major turning point in the war. By December the Allies had carried out a successful invasion in West Africa and the Nazi invasion of the Soviet Union had been stymied at Stalingrad. Any thought of further cooperation with the Germans was out of the question, although opposition to the British continued.

Nasser set himself to the difficult task of strengthening the Free Officers' movement.

As it became evident that the Allies were going to defeat Germany and Japan, the Free Officers were instructed to arouse sentiment against the British in any way possible. At the same time, Nasser took every precaution to keep the Free Officers from being detected. The group was organized into small, isolated cells of up to five men each. A member had contact only with the other men of his cell, thus eliminating the danger that he would name the entire group under questioning by the police. Nasser's reading and experience had convinced him that most plots were wrecked through the capture of secret documents, so very little was committed to paper. The Free Officers' organizational structure, membership, times and places of meetings — all were kept in Nasser's head.

Such methods ensure the consolidation of power in the leader, as only the leader knows all of the group's workings. In the early days of the war, while Nasser was in the Sudan, Sadat and other close associates of Nasser, such as Abdel Hakim Amer, had carried out their own plans. Sadat had even been jailed for his scheming with the Nazis. By the end of the war, Nasser was the indisputable leader of the Free Officers' movement. To those, like Sadat, who advocated terrorism to hasten Egypt's independence, Nasser advised patience. He firmly believed that only when the Free Officers had consolidated their support within the military could their movement be successful. Their day would come.

> *[The Free Officers] had in common not an ideology, but a common determination to reform Egypt.*
> —DEREK HOPWOOD
> British historian

3

The Free Officers

Nasser had been promoted to captain shortly before El Alamein, and about six months later he was made an instructor at the Military Academy. While teaching, he continued his own military and political studies. More important, he found himself in a position in which he could screen young cadets, an opportunity he used to recruit men into the Free Officers group. He would carefully and discreetly feel them out, judging their potential as revolutionaries. In this way the ranks of the Free Officers grew, and Nasser began organizing them into units with special functions. The Free Officers group became a well-run military organization. Nasser also made contacts with Marxist groups and the Muslim Brotherhood, who were the other primary opposition groups within Egypt.

In 1943 Nasser married Tahia Kazem, the sister of a friend. In traditional Arab fashion, Tahia stayed very much in the background during Nasser's career and was rarely seen in public. They had five children.

> [F]or him who waits, tomorrow
> is close.
> —NASSER

Nasser and his wife, Tahia, were married in 1943, while he was an instructor at the military academy. In traditional Arab fashion, he kept his wife, and later his children, in the background, away from his public life.

UPI/BETTMANN NEWSPHOTOS

King Farouk (left) raises the Egyptian flag at a 1947 ceremony marking the end of the British military presence in Egypt. Nasser and the Free Officers regarded Britain's refusal to withdraw its troops around the Suez Canal as intolerable and continued to oppose the British.

The end of World War II left Egypt in a fragile political state. Nationalist feelings ran high, and the country was even more divided along economic lines. While war profits had swollen the bank accounts of the upper classes, the resulting inflation had been hard on the working class, and sudden industrial cutbacks at the war's end left 300,000 unemployed.

The war's end left thousands of British troops in Alexandria and Cairo. Many Egyptians resented the troops, as their presence was a violation of the treaty of 1936, which restricted the British military presence to the Suez Canal zone. Fierce rioting occurred in the first months of the year. The Muslim Brotherhood escalated their campaign to rid Egypt of foreign influence, advocating a total boycott of all things British and threatening to unleash their terrorist wing. Sadat organized an assassination of a former cabinet minister who had advocated "eternal cooperation with England." Prime ministers came and went, all compromised in the eyes of the opposition and the populace because of their perceived willingness to compromise with Britain.

In May 1946 the British government proposed the withdrawal of all British forces from Egypt. On July 4, 1946, a British general presented the Egyptian chief of staff with the key to the city of Cairo, a symbolic gesture of the British withdrawal.

Some of the Free Officers argued that their work was done, but Nasser disagreed. The British still kept troops in the canal zone, so vital to their commercial and colonial interests. As long as the British maintained their presence there, the Free Officers would continue their efforts.

Nasser had been admitted to a two-year program of further training at the Army Staff College in 1946. While there his attention was drawn by events in Palestine, the region to Egypt's northeast, bordered to the north by Syria and Lebanon, to the east by the Jordan River, the Dead Sea, and Transjordan, and on the west by the Mediterranean. Palestine had been the homeland of the Jews, most of whom were driven from the area by the Romans in the first and second centuries, after the destruction of Jerusalem in A.D. 70. In the intervening years the land had largely been settled by Arabs, though some Jews had remained there. Beginning in the late 19th century, the Zionist movement gained impetus. Zionism advocated the return of the Jews from the diaspora — as the settling of the Jews outside Palestine is known — to their ancient homeland of Palestine and the establishment of a Jewish state.

The peace negotiations that ended World War I placed Palestine, which had been under the control of the defeated Ottoman Empire, under a British mandate. The Zionist movement gathered momentum in 1917 with the Balfour Declaration, a letter by British Foreign Secretary Arthur Balfour declaring British support for the establishment of a Jewish homeland in Palestine. Jews emigrated to Palestine in great numbers in the next three decades. The Jewish population there increased from 60,000 in 1914 to 700,000 in 1948.

Arabs in Palestine and the surrounding areas were not pleased by these events. They regarded Palestine as their own and viewed British support of Zionism as a betrayal, since during World War I they had fought with the British against the Ottoman Turks. Arab guerrillas attacked Jewish settlements. As World War II approached Britain restricted Jewish immigration to Palestine in an attempt to placate the still numerically superior Arab population. Several militant Jewish organizations within Palestine waged a terrorist campaign designed to force the British hand — and began putting in place the framework for an independent government.

The decision of the United Nations (UN) to partition Palestine into separate Arab and Jewish states brought angry demonstrations in Cairo and other Arab cities. Both the Jews and the Arabs living there regarded Palestine as their homeland.

Jews in Palestine proclaimed the establishment of the independent state of Israel in May 1948, immediately after the British withdrawal. The 1949 UN Security Council vote admitting Israel as a General Assembly member (pictured) was an implicit rejection of the Arab refusal to recognize Israel's right to exist.

The British relinquished their mandate to the newly formed United Nations in 1946 and announced that they would withdraw their troops on May 15, 1948. In November 1947 the United Nations decided to partition Palestine into separate Jewish and Arab states. The Arab world loudly denounced the plan. In Cairo, as in the other states of the Arab League, which had been formed to oppose the establishment of a Jewish nation in Palestine, street demonstrators demanded that the Arab countries take action. When the Jewish settlers declared the establishment of the state of Israel on May 15, 1948, Egypt, Syria, Lebanon, Iraq, and Transjordan (now Jordan) immediately declared war.

When war broke out Nasser was recently finished with his advanced training, now a major and a commanding officer. On May 16 he left for the front, hopeful that the Egyptian army could restore some of the nation's lost pride with a smashing victory over the Israelis. However, the ill-trained and poorly led Egyptian army was not to acquit itself well. Later he wrote of his initial experiences in the war:

> Our apprehensions began when we arrived at El Arish, one of the main bases behind the front lines. . . . We did not even know the whereabouts of the unit we were to join, and no one was there to show us. We headed for the HQ, expecting to find a beehive bursting with activity: it was deserted. It was like a forgotten house in a region abandoned by everyone.

The rest of the campaign in Palestine was a similar mix of disorganization and bad military planning. Nasser finally found his unit, the Sixth Brigade, which proceeded into Gaza, a strip of land along the coast between Palestine and Egypt. There it sustained heavy casualties in battle with the Israelis. Afterward Nasser visited the camp hospital and was sickened by the sight of wounded and mutilated soldiers. As the disastrous Palestine campaign progressed, his resentment against the Egyptian high command grew and grew. As he later wrote: "How I despised those rookie generals, relaxing in their armchairs, totally unaware of what a battlefield is like, totally unaware of the sufferings of the combatants, and content to place an idle finger on the map and order that such-and-such a position be taken."

The United Nations arranged a cease-fire, which was only partially observed by both sides. The truce finally fell apart on July 8, and thereafter the Israelis never lost momentum, driving the Arab forces back on all fronts. The Arab effort was plagued by shortages of weapons and supplies, and the total lack of coordination between the various countries' forces all but guaranteed defeat. By the end of 1948 one of the few pockets of resistance left was an Egyptian brigade near the town of Faluja in Palestine's south-

The Israeli flag is displayed at its London consulate following Great Britain's recognition of the nation in 1949. Jews around the world celebrated the establishment of Israel as the realization of their dreams of a homeland in the Holy Land.

The defeat of the Arabs in the war accompanying the establishment of Israel led to the displacement of thousands of Arabs who had made their home in Palestine. Known as Palestinians, their desire for a homeland remains an unresolved issue that has continued to divide the Middle East.

ern desert, the Negev. Nasser was among the commanders at Faluja. He was wounded early in the battle and was evacuated to a Cairo hospital, but after recuperating he insisted on returning to the front, where he led a counterattack that enabled the battered Egyptian forces to hold out until an Israeli-Egyptian truce was signed in February 1949. For Nasser and his men the war was over, but the experience left a bitter taste that lasted for the rest of his life.

"We were fighting in Palestine," he later wrote, "but our dreams were centered in Egypt."

The war had been an almost total defeat for the Arabs. One of the few things to survive the war intact was Nasser's own professional reputation. Even the Israeli military chiefs saluted Nasser's courage and command ability, and his fame spread throughout Egypt.

Nasser felt anything but a hero. Humiliation after humiliation had been heaped on Egypt, made weak by decades of colonial rule, and to Nasser the pain was almost unbearable. The war had done little but reveal the total incompetence of the army command and the criminal negligence of the Egyptian government. It was common knowledge that the supply shortages had occurred chiefly because of corrupt procurement procedures within the government bureaucracy. The weapons that were sent to the front had proven hopelessly and sometimes lethally inadequate. Antique rifles had jammed, grenades had exploded in the hands of soldiers who were about to throw them — it had been a debacle all around, an embarrassment to every Egyptian.

After the first Arab-Israeli war Nasser's perspective shifted. Until then the aim of the revolution had been simply to remove the British. Now he saw that this would not be enough. The entire society had grown corrupt — the military, the government, the British, the large landowners who exploited the landless peasantry — all had weakened Egyptian society and were equally to blame for the devastating defeat.

Like most Egyptians, Nasser had never been enamored of the monarchy but had at least acknowledged the king as a symbol of Egyptian sovereignty.

The establishment of the independent state of Israel brought an immediate declaration of war from five Arab states — Egypt, Transjordan, Syria, Iraq, and Lebanon. Nasser fought with the Egyptian troops. The decisive defeat of the Arabs further convinced him that a revolution was necessary to revitalize Egypt.

Egyptian peasants carry live-stock home from market. Most of Egypt's peasants were subsistence farmers who cultivated less than a half acre of land apiece. King Farouk's opulent life-style, womanizing, and vast fortune disenchanted many in a country suffering from widespread poverty.

However, King Farouk had become a tarnished symbol. His capitulation to the British during World War II had compromised him in the eyes of the nationalists. His notorious reputation as a gambler and womanizer angered fundamentalist Muslims. His divorce of his first wife by royal decree infuriated Egyptian women. In a land in which many peasants had less than a half acre from which to eke out a living, the king owned 20 percent of the arable land and had amassed a fortune estimated at $580 million. He built himself lavish palaces and kept a fleet of over two hundred automobiles. What most enraged Nasser was the corruption the monarchy engendered — corruption that allowed members of the government to siphon off funds that were intended to buy modern weapons for the army in Israel. When Nasser determined that the monarchy had to go, he was able to draw upon the rising tide of discontent with Farouk.

The most immediate task was the reorganization of the Free Officers. There were holes in the ranks — comrades who had fallen in combat — and new recruits were needed. As the conspiracy grew, tighter security was required. Both the British and the Egyptian bureaucracy were aware there was a conspiracy afoot somewhere, but no one was sure where. Years later even some who had been a part of the Free Officers' movement were surprised to learn that Nasser was the leader.

Nasser's group grew bold enough to proclaim its own existence through the publishing and distribution of several pamphlets. In 1950 these pamphlets were turned into an underground newspaper called the *Voice of the Free Officers*. The actual identity of the Free Officers still remained a closely guarded secret. One of the first pamphlets was entitled "The Army Gives a Warning" and denounced Farouk and the corruption that had been responsible for providing the Egyptian soldiers with defective weapons during the war with Israel. Shortly afterward a member of parliament similarly denounced the corruption of the Farouk regime, as did one of Cairo's weekly, mainstream newspapers, whose editor was jailed for his efforts. These events indicated that far from propagating an extremist viewpoint, the Free Officers were expressing feelings shared by many in Egyptian society.

Farouk sought to deflect the growing discontent by holding free elections in 1950. The Wafd were still Egypt's most popular party and won a majority. Mustafa Nahas was once again appointed prime minister. It was evident that the majority of Egyptians were no longer satisfied with moderate measures. The Muslim Brotherhood continued to grow in strength. Nahas's wife was implicated in a cotton market scandal that resulted in hefty profits for herself and two associates. It seemed the Nahas government was tainted by the same sort of corruption as infected the monarchy. Unemployment rose.

Nahas and the Wafd majority in parliament decided to take advantage of the widespread unrest by focusing it on a longtime target, the British. In October 1951 the parliament declared that the 1936 treaty with Great Britain, which Nahas and the Wafd had played a large part in implementing, was no longer in effect.

The action was tantamount to a declaration of war, as in abrogating the treaty Nahas had made the presence of British troops in the canal zone and the Sudan illegal. The Wafd demanded an immediate British evacuation. The Muslim Brotherhood and other militant groups immediately organized guerrilla bands to harass the British installations around the Suez Canal. The British denounced the parliamentary move and reinforced their positions in the region.

Nasser was of two minds about these developments. Although he applauded the parliament's action, he feared that events might force the Free Officers to act before it was wise to do so. Nasser had carefully and patiently built up his movement over the years, and he felt the effort still needed time. Indeed, in 1949 he had laid out a long-term plan for the conspiracy's success, with a target year of 1954. He did not relish the thought of again plunging his men into action unprepared, as he had been forced to do in Palestine, but events were forcing him to move more quickly than planned.

Down with joint defense and with any collective security pact under imperialism.
—from a Free Officers's pamphlet objecting to British military presence in Egypt

4

The Dawn of Freedom

On Friday, January 25, 1952, British artillery leveled an Egyptian police barracks in Ismailia, near the Suez Canal. This punitive action, which left 50 Egyptians dead and 100 wounded, was taken in retaliation for months of guerrilla attacks against British troops. Ten days before, guerrilla commandos had blown up a large munitions depot, killing ten British soldiers. British authorities charged the Ismailia police with aiding the guerrillas.

The next day Cairo went up in flames. Angry mobs set torches to places that were considered embodiments of foreign and upper-class oppression — theaters, expensive department stores, stylish restaurants, hotels that catered to foreigners (and barred Egyptians), foreign banks and other foreign businesses — all while the police, for the most part, looked on approvingly. Entire blocks of downtown Cairo burned to the ground.

It was clear to Nasser that events were overtaking his five-year plan. The time for revolution had arrived. The stage was set.

The Revolution of July 23 marks the realization of the hope held by the people of Egypt since they began, in modern times, to think of self-government and complete sovereignty.
—NASSER

The Egyptian revolution began in earnest in January 1952 with riots in Cairo and the burning of upper-class and foreign commercial establishments that symbolized colonial domination of Egypt.

English-language signs are replaced with Arabic signs in Cairo. The prevalence of English, in addition to being representative of the British domination of Egypt, made it necessary for Egyptians to learn English in order to be literate in their own country.

At this time the Free Officers could claim over 150 members, many of whom were still quite young. But Nasser feared that the Free Officers, once they made their bid for power, might be perceived as a gang of rebellious young upstarts — not quite the image that would lend credibility to the revolution. Nasser and the Executive Committee — as the conspiracy's leadership was called — searched for a suitable symbolic figure to play the role of leader, someone who would be respected and taken seriously. The man they settled on was Major General Mohammed Naguib. Naguib was a veteran of the Palestine war, and although he was not widely known to the public, he was sympathetic to the conspiracy's aims and was an excellent commanding officer. He had first attracted Nasser's attention when he offered his resignation from the army after the humiliating incident when the British surrounded the royal palace during World War II. Above all, Naguib was in his fifties. Age is respected in the Muslim world, perhaps more so than in the West. Nasser thought that Naguib would make a very good front man. He approached Naguib and found the general more than willing to take the job. As it turned out Naguib was to prove something more than a figurehead.

Nasser decided that the Free Officers would strike at the beginning of August, but events moved more quickly than he had anticipated. On July 20 he learned that Farouk was planning to establish a new government, with his friends in high cabinet posts. Worse, he was planning to arrest Nasser and other Free Officers. The decision was made to act within 48 hours.

On the night of July 22, 1952, more than 2,500 years of bondage ended. The Free Officers carried out their long-awaited change of government with characteristic efficiency. Little was left to chance.

"We have 99 chances out of 100 of succeeding," Nasser assured a comrade in the early stages.

The continued British military presence in the Suez Canal zone angered the Egyptians, as this effigy of a British soldier hung over a Cairo street in January 1952 indicates. The sign reads "gallows awaits the necks of the British"; guerrilla attacks on the troops were common.

The coup d'état occurred late at night. Commanded by Free Officers, columns of armored cars and tanks rumbled through the streets of Cairo, all converging on the army general headquarters. Evidently the high command knew of the coup but could do nothing to prevent it. Nasser had placed his men in strategic posts throughout the Egyptian army. Every countermove the generals could think of was blocked. Nasser's handpicked men took command of key army, air force, cavalry, and artillery units throughout Egypt and the Sinai Peninsula, all the way to the Israeli border. An armored column was sent to block the road to the canal zone in order to intercept any British units trying to intervene.

British troops keep Egyptian soldiers under the gun at Ismailia, near the Suez Canal, where repeated Egyptian guerrilla harassment led to the destruction of an Egyptian police barracks by British artillery in January 1952, leaving 150 Egyptians dead or wounded. The incident triggered the burning of Cairo the next day.

All went according to plan. The Free Officers were pleasantly surprised to find that a substantial majority of non-conspiracy officers and enlisted men supported the coup. By 1:00 A.M. the armed forces had taken over radio stations, telegraph offices, police stations, and key government buildings. Except for two sentries at army headquarters who had been killed, the coup was bloodless.

At 7:00 A.M. the government radio station went on the air with a news bulletin. "In the name of General Mohammed Naguib," the announcement said, "the armed forces of the nation have seized control of the government in order to restore the honor of the Egyptian people."

The burning of Cairo was not, though it may seem so today, a simple criminal episode, but an explosion by those who had nothing against those who monopolized the very right to live.
—MOHAMMED HASSANEIN HEYKAL
spokesman for the
Free Officers

UPI/BETTMANN NEWSPHOTOS

The corruption of Farouk (pictured) convinced Nasser that the king, as well as the British, had to be removed. The news that Farouk was planning to act against the Free Officers led Nasser to move the date of the coup forward.

It had been surprisingly easy, but now that the Free Officers held power, it remained to be seen how they would implement their somewhat abstract plans for social reform. The Executive Committee had long ago drawn up a six-point statement of principles, but aside from specifically setting forth the goal of ridding Egypt of British troops and British influence, the statement was rather vague on social and political issues. It called for the "liquidation of feudalism" and for putting an end to the "domination of the power of capital." It also spoke of establishing "social equality" and "a healthy democratic life" but said nothing about how this was to be accomplished.

At a press conference that morning, Naguib was similarly vague about the aims of the Free Officers. He did state that Farouk would have to go and announced their intention to reinstate the constitution and have Aly Maher, a longtime politician and foe of the British whose appointment as prime minister had triggered the crisis of February 4, 1942, return as prime minister.

Meanwhile, foreign governments, particularly the British, were scrambling to learn the political orientation of the Free Officers, who ran the gamut of political opinion. Nasser himself was a political pragmatist and belonged to no clearly definable political camp at that time. While he flatly rejected communism as a social doctrine, he had maintained contact with communists within Egypt. On the other hand he also distrusted capitalism, which he held responsible for the inequities in the distribution of wealth that made possible the great contrast between the rich, like Farouk and his cronies, and the great majority of poor Egyptians. His goal was to forge a compromise between the two. At this point, however, the details of this vision were not very clear. This mattered little to the foreign observers, as no one aside from the Free Officers themselves knew that it was Nasser who was the leader.

Before broader social and political questions could be considered there were a number of immediate tasks to attend to. The Executive Committee was converted into the Revolutionary Command

Council (RCC) and given broad powers. The RCC immediately called for a restoration of the 1923 constitution, the abolition of censorship, the disbanding of the monarchy's secret police, the release of political prisoners, and, most important, the abdication of the king.

The coup had been timed to coincide with Farouk's departure to Alexandria for the summer. Sadat and Naguib and two armored divisions were sent to Alexandria. Some members of the Free Officers argued that Farouk should be put to death, but Nasser felt that an execution would only lead to further bloodshed. The king was allowed to abdicate in favor of his son, Ahmad Fuad, who was still an infant. He left Egypt for Italy and permanent exile on July 25.

The next item on the agenda was removing British troops from the canal zone. The RCC undertook a series of diplomatic offensives. At this time the United States showed signs of being sympathetic to the new Egyptian regime. Nasser hoped that the United States could use its influence to convince the British to leave. He also told U.S. diplomats that Egypt needed military and economic aid. The United States was willing to supply arms only if Egypt joined the North Atlantic Treaty Organization (NATO), the western military alliance against the Soviet Union, of which Great Britain was also a member. Nasser balked at this — it would mean that Egypt and Britain would be allies.

> *If we were to evacuate the Canal Zone before making a Middle East defence arrangement we should be exposing ourselves to Egyptian blackmail.*
> —ANTHONY EDEN
> British prime minister
> (1955–57)

The Free Officers seized control of the government late on the night of July 22, 1952. Two days later tanks and soldiers surrounded the royal palace in Alexandria (pictured) and forced Farouk to abdicate and leave the country.

Nasser's diplomatic overtures had little effect on the British, who were very nervous about Egypt's accepting U.S. arms and stalled talks on pulling out of the canal zone. With diplomatic solutions exhausted, the RCC authorized a resumption of guerrilla harassment.

On June 18, 1953, at Nasser's order, Egypt was officially declared a republic, with Naguib as its president and prime minister. Everyone in the government knew power still resided with the RCC and Nasser — everyone except Naguib, that is. The general was enjoying his role as the nation's leader and was beginning to think of himself as something more than a figurehead. He had support among many politicians, and the Egyptian masses liked his quiet, reassuring charm.

The impending rift between Naguib and Nasser was hinted at by Nasser's refusal to allow Naguib to be named the commander in chief of the military. The position went instead to Abdel Hakim Amer, one of Nasser's oldest and most trusted associates. Nasser named himself minister of the interior, responsible for maintaining domestic security and rooting out opposition. Quietly, censorship was imposed. Telephones were tapped. Those suspected of being opponents of the revolution were arrested and detained without trial.

Nasser and Naguib soon came into conflict over domestic policy. Nasser believed that Egypt had to undergo two revolutions simultaneously. The political revolution had been accomplished in part, but the social revolution had not yet begun. The machinery of land redistribution had been outlined but not yet implemented.

The Egyptian landholding and agricultural system was characterized by vast inequality. About 2000 families owned most of the country's productive land, which they leased to the peasants at exorbitant rates while making huge profits from the sale of crops grown by the peasants. Nasser planned to strip these large landowners of any property over 200 *feddan* (a feddan is roughly equal to an acre), which would still produce an average yearly income of $60,000. The government would buy the excess land and sell it to the fellahin, the peasantry, in plots of up to five feddan, at terms the peasants could manage. At the time, the average annual income of a peasant was $40.

Naguib was reluctant to proceed hastily with any large-scale reforms. According to Naguib, the army had no business governing now that the revolution had been successful. He favored an immediate return to parliamentary government and an end to censorship and arrests. Nasser believed such steps opened the door to counterrevolution. What good did it do to get rid of a corrupt monarch if the politicians who served him were left to continue their old corrupt ways? The Egyptian masses must be

Nasser (front, second from left) and Mohammed Naguib (front, third from left) with other members of the Revolutionary Command Council (RCC), the new government of Egypt after the revolt of the Free Officers. Naguib was chosen by Nasser to be the figurehead leader of the revolution and became president and prime minister.

delivered from exploitation at the hands of a privileged few. This was what social revolution was all about.

The RCC backed Nasser. Naguib resigned in protest in February 1954, and the RCC proclaimed Nasser the new prime minister. However, Nasser was chagrined to find that he lacked the necessary support to make his position stick. He had underestimated Naguib's powers of persuasion. Nasser was seen by his opponents as a hothead, an upstart, a burgeoning military dictator. University students staged demonstrations protesting army rule, and even some units of the army itself favored Naguib over Nasser.

Nasser also had supporters in the army and in the population at large, but age temporarily won out

Waving the flag of the revolution, Egyptian peasants salute Naguib, who was popularly hailed as the hero of the rebellion. Nasser's role as the leader of the Free Officers was little known, although he wielded the true power in the newly formed government.

over youth. Rather than split the army into opposing factions and risk civil war, Nasser backed down and agreed to share power with Naguib. Naguib was reinstated as prime minister, and Nasser resumed his post as deputy prime minister. Nasser was not satisfied with this title. Large-scale, meaningful land reform looked as though it would be undercut by the old politicians, who would soon be back in power. But all was not lost. Nasser was by now a master of conspiracy, and he proceeded to engineer another coup.

Nasser's clever ploy was simply to let things slide. The RCC announced that it would dissolve itself after the elections. All political parties would be allowed complete freedom. The RCC would not interfere. A new government would be in power by July

As Naguib (left) took a more active leadership role, he clashed with Nasser (right) over land reform, the role of the military in government, and free elections. Naguib was forced from power and Nasser was recognized as Egypt's undisputed leader.

1954. If things went as expected, the old, familiar faces would be back, and they would be around for a long time to come.

Naguib had been outflanked. Egyptians had no desire to return to the days before the revolution. Trade unions called general strikes, demonstrators — some of them paid by Nasser — took to the streets, and progressive newspapers published blistering editorials denouncing a return to the bad old days before the RCC.

Nasser carefully orchestrated this coordinated attack, backed by his army loyalists. As before Nasser proved to be a superior chess player; his pieces were better positioned than his opponent's. Naguib was neutralized and had to resign as prime minister, though he retained the powerless position of president. His supporters protested, but their king had been checkmated and the game was over. Nasser's position as Egypt's leader was now secure. The next task was dealing with the British.

5

War in Suez

Guerrilla attacks on British bases in the canal zone had continued during the struggle between Nasser and Naguib. In May of 1954 Nasser called off the raids and resumed negotiations with London. He knew that Egypt lacked the military power to dislodge the British and hoped that what could not be done by brute force might be accomplished through clever negotiation. Nasser negotiated.

On October 19, 1954, Egypt and Britain signed a treaty that provided for the withdrawal of all British military units from Egyptian territory by July 1956. The canal zone installations would be jointly manned by Egyptian soldiers and British technicians in civilian dress. Britain dropped its insistence that Egypt join NATO and suggested a limited alliance that would allow British soldiers back in the country if Egypt were attacked.

> *The canal has never ceased to cause suffering to the people who dug it.*
> —HUSSEIN FAWZI
> Egyptian author

As the sole leader of the most populous Arab country, Nasser was naturally a powerful figure in the Arab world; his determination to revitalize Egypt without Western interference and his actions during the Suez crisis increased his influence.

UPI/BETTMANN NEWSPHOTOS

UPI/BETTMANN NEWSPHOTOS

Nasser presides over a meeting of the RCC. Anwar Sadat is at right, second from bottom. Hoping to negotiate a British withdrawal from the Suez Canal zone, Nasser and the RCC ordered an end to guerrilla raids on British military bases there in May 1954.

There were objections from militant quarters. The Muslim Brotherhood called the treaty a betrayal, as it in effect allied Egypt with the non-Islamic West. Some extremists went beyond verbal protest. Shortly after the treaty was signed a member of the Muslim Brotherhood fired at Nasser during a mass rally in Alexandria. The shots went wild, and the gunman was apprehended. Nasser used the incident as an excuse to crack down on extremists. More than 1,000 Brotherhood members were jailed and 6 were hanged for treason. Naguib was implicated in an alleged plot by the Brotherhood to assassinate the entire RCC and was arrested. The days of bloodless victory were over, but the most dangerous opposition forces had been eliminated.

With the military-political revolution an accomplished fact, Nasser turned his attention to the social revolution. His land reform was proceeding slowly. By 1954 only a few peasant families had acquired land, and it would be well into the 1960s before a substantial percentage of the land was redistributed. Nasser had discovered that secret plots and sudden military takeovers were one thing, and social revolutions another. Through land reform the landed class was transforming itself into a capitalist class by investing the money they received for their land in lucrative new businesses. The gap between rich and poor had not been narrowed, and Nasser was forced to think of other ways to accomplish his social revolution. In time his thinking on domestic policy would swing to the left. He would come to prefer planned economies and government-owned industries as opposed to free-market economies and private enterprise.

A convoy sails through the Suez Canal at its opening in November 1869. Although Britain cherished control over the canal as vital to its commercial and colonial interests, Egypt under Nasser regarded continued British control as an intolerable reminder of its colonial past.

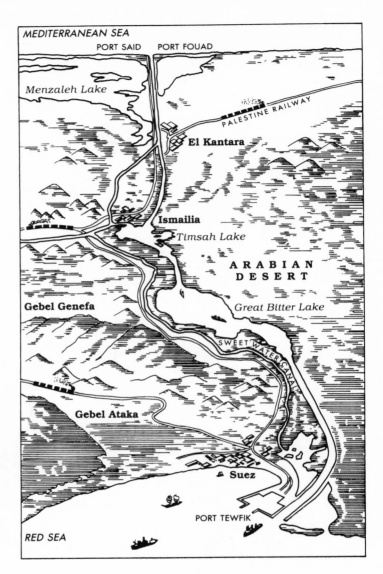

The Suez Canal connects the Mediterranean Sea to the Red Sea and provides a greatly shortened route for shipping between Europe and Asia. Britain gained control of the strategic waterway in 1875 when the bankruptcy of his government forced Ismail Pasha to sell Egypt's shares in the canal.

In foreign policy Nasser tried to remain neutral despite a slow but steady drift in his thinking away from the West. Egypt's continued military weakness had been exposed in August 1955 when an Israeli commando raid into Egyptian territory had killed 35 Egyptians. Nasser desperately needed arms to bolster his country's military position against Israel. He wanted to deal with the West, but neither Britain nor the United States would make good on assurances to sell him weapons. Egyptian neutrality apparently was not good enough; the administration of President Dwight D. Eisenhower wanted staunch allies in the Middle East and wanted Egypt to join a defense alliance similar to NATO. Nasser, who did not want close ties with any non-Arab country, nonetheless decided to turn to the Soviet Union for the weapons his army needed.

The Soviet Union had been a world power since World War II, when it had been one of the victorious Allies. As a global power with widespread interests to promote and protect, the Soviet Union gladly offered Nasser all the tanks, jet fighters, and jet bombers he wanted in exchange for Egyptian cotton. Nasser made last-minute attempts to persuade the United States and Britain that he was serious about dealing with the Soviet Union — to no avail. Nasser signed the Soviet arms agreement in September 1955.

Nasser relaxes with two British diplomats, Anthony Nutting (left) and Sir Ralph Stevenson (right) in October 1954 after signing a treaty providing for the gradual withdrawal of British troops from around the Suez Canal. The treaty was regarded as a sell-out by hard-liners within Egypt.

American reaction was predictably critical. U.S. foreign policy experts in the Eisenhower administration feared that behind Nasser's claims of neutrality lay a deep hostility to the United States. But Secretary of State John Foster Dulles was determined not to let Egypt fall into the Soviet camp and recommended that the United States consider extending the economic aid that Nasser wanted.

In addition to arms, Egypt needed more irrigated farmland to feed a swiftly growing population. Nasser proposed building a dam near the town of Aswan

An angry crowd in Cairo burned the headquarters of the Muslim Brotherhood, a militant Islamic group, following an attempt by one of its members to assassinate Nasser in October 1954. The group opposed Nasser's Suez Canal treaty with Britain. Nasser cracked down on domestic opposition after the attempt.

in southern Egypt. Through the centuries farming had been made possible by the yearly flooding of the Nile, which irrigated the nearby lands. These floods were also often destructive, however. The dam at Aswan would eliminate flooding by holding water in a huge lake behind the dam. Water would then be run off as needed, providing year-round irrigation. Because farmers would no longer have to depend on the flood season, more than one crop per year could be grown.

Eager to earn Egyptian goodwill at the expense of

> *The canal—which our history books present to us as a considerable asset made available to Egypt by the European enterprising spirit and technical genius—was seen by almost all Egyptians as a mortgage on their independence.*
> —JEAN LACOUTURE
> Nasser biographer

Egyptians rallied around Nasser following the Suez Canal treaty with Britain and the attempt on his life. Although many opposed the provisions of the treaty that allowed Britain to return its troops should Egypt be attacked, Nasser was revered for having rid Egypt of Farouk and the British.

the Soviets, without having to provide weapons, the United States and Britain were willing to underwrite the Aswan project. The American-controlled World Bank was prepared to lend Egypt $200 million to initiate work on the dam, but the offer brought with it stringent conditions. Egypt had to practice fiscal responsibility and curb inflation, consult with the United States and Britain on important budgetary matters, and accept no other foreign aid — especially from the Soviet Union.

At first Nasser balked. He viewed the conditions as nothing short of imperialist meddling in Egyp-

tian affairs. Aware that it was a massive foreign debt and government bankruptcy that had provided the pretext for the extensive European interference in Egyptian affairs in the 19th century, Nasser was understandably wary of a loan with too many strings attached. But when he began to fear that the United States would withdraw the offer, he swallowed Egypt's pride and withdrew his objections to the proposal.

However the United States reneged on the Aswan dam project, citing the "weakness of the Egyptian economy" and the "instability of the regime." Dulles

Nasser raises the Egyptian flag over Camp Shalufa, the first British Army base in the Suez Canal zone to be handed over to Egypt under the 1954 treaty.

was also hesitant to support Nasser because of his willingness to deal with the Soviets and in July 1956 scotched the Aswan deal.

Nasser's next move sent shocks throughout the Western world. In a July 26 speech in Alexandria, Nasser announced that Egypt would take complete control of the Suez Canal, which was still owned by British and French interests. The nationalization of the canal would occur immediately; even as Nasser spoke, Egyptian soldiers entered the offices of the Suez Company and placed them under government authority. All canal revenue would go to finance the Aswan dam.

It was a bold and dangerous move. Nasser figured he had at least two months to settle the crisis diplomatically before Britain could mount a military expedition to retake the canal. He did not expect France or the United States to do anything.

The Arab world applauded the move, and overnight Nasser became the leading champion of Arab nationalism and independence. The majority of Egyptians looked upon the canal as both a blessing and a curse. Built with foreign money, foreign expertise, and the sweat — and sometimes the blood — of poor Egyptians, the Suez Canal had served as an excuse for decades of foreign occupation. In effect it had mortgaged Egypt's independence. Only by establishing total Egyptian control could this curse be removed.

Nasser had not bargained on the severity of British and French reaction to the seizure of the canal. Sir Anthony Eden, Britain's prime minister, denounced Nasser, calling him a dangerous dictator. The French were equally upset, and 18 of the canal's 45 user countries issued a joint statement calling for the return of the canal to international control.

Nasser and Soviet leader Nikita Khrushchev in 1958. Nasser turned to the Soviet Union after the United States rebuffed his requests for military and economic aid, although Egypt remained neutral.

Nasser with U.S. president Dwight Eisenhower in 1960. The United States became sensitive to the importance of Egypt as a vital Middle East nation only after Nasser signed an arms agreement with the Soviet Union in July 1955.

Nasser stood fast, saying he would not relinquish Egyptian control of the canal. At the same time, however, he sent out peace feelers, hoping that the crisis could still be solved diplomatically. Nasser was willing to compromise, to a degree. In fact he hoped for a settlement from the outset — one favorable to Egypt to be sure, but a peaceful settlement all the same.

Nasser felt sure that neither Britain nor France had enough military forces stationed in the Middle East to conduct an effective military campaign. Further, he could not bring himself to believe that either country would enter into a joint action with Israel to recapture the canal. Such a venture, he felt, would be insane, a move guaranteed to outrage the Arab world and forever nullify French and British influence in the Middle East.

Yet Nasser had badly miscalculated. Israel was particularly eager to strike against him. In recent months Nasser's influence in the Arab world had grown. Egyptian guerrillas continued to carry out raids within Israel. Meanwhile, Nasser had begun giving radio speeches, broadcast widely throughout the Arab world, in which he denounced Britain and Israel. Within Jordan, Israel's neighbor to the east, the Palestinians — those Arabs who had been displaced by the creation of the state of Israel — were particularly influenced by Nasser's message. The Palestinians also carried out widespread guerrilla and terrorist activities against Israel. The recent election of a pro-Egyptian parliament within that nation created a further element of anti-Israel unrest. Incensed by the Baghdad Pact, a mutual defense treaty signed by Iraq, Turkey, and Great Britain in early 1955, Nasser called on all Arab nations to put aside their differences, realize their common interests, and unite against the West and Israel. Nasser's message of pan-Arabism aroused Israel's fears of destruction at the hands of the united Arab nations. Within Israel there had been talk of war against Egypt for some time. The Suez crisis provided a welcome opportunity for such a strike, particularly if the British and French were to assist.

A Soviet freighter passes disabled ships in the Suez Canal in early 1957. Nasser ordered ships scuttled in the canal to render it useless in the face of the British, French, and Israeli invasion following his nationalization of the waterway in July 1956.

French participation was less directly connected to Nasser's nationalization of the canal than to the threat his regime posed to French interests in the Middle East and North Africa, particularly in Algeria, where a war of independence against French colonial rule had been going on since 1954. Nasser supplied weapons and aid to the rebel forces there.

The British, of course, sought to intervene to recover their lost revenues from the canal but also to further their interests in other parts of the Arab world where they sought to maintain an influence, particularly Jordan and Iraq. Nasser's constant barrage of anti-British propaganda made maintaining such interests increasingly difficult.

Port Said, Egypt, following a British bombing raid before the 1956 invasion. Nasser underestimated the extent to which Britain would go to reclaim the canal and the enmity his aggressive Arab nationalism had aroused in France and Israel.

On October 29, 1956, Israeli armored forces rolled into the Gaza Strip and swept out over the Sinai Peninsula, pushing ill-prepared Egyptian units back over a wide and rapidly receding front. The Israelis crossed the Sinai in three days, stopping on the east bank of the Suez Canal. On October 31 British Canberra bombers attacked Egyptian airfields, destroying many of the Russian planes that made up Egypt's brand-new air force. Most of the pilots had not yet learned to fly the new planes.

A combined Anglo-French force landed at Port Said in the canal zone. There the European forces met surprising resistance from armed Egyptian civilians. Still, Egypt was outmatched.

[Nasser] was the symbol of the overall struggle against Western domination and the takeover of the Canal was symbolic of the gradual reclamation by the Arabs of their heritage.
—DEREK HOPWOOD
British historian

The Soviet Union flatly rejected Nasser's plea for help, occupied as they were with events in Eastern Europe, where the Hungarians had revolted against Soviet domination. As Moscow ordered tanks into the streets of Budapest, the Hungarian capital, the Suez Canal remained far from the minds of Kremlin strategists. The Soviet Union would not go to war over Suez. Though outraged by the invasion, the United States could not very well wage war against its greatest European allies. No Arab nation was in a position to provide assistance. Nasser stood alone, hoping that world opinion would turn the tide.

Indeed, most of the world was shocked that great powers such as Britain and France would wage open warfare against helpless Egypt. Diplomatic pressure forced Eden to declare a cease-fire before the invading forces could consolidate their positions. The United States demanded immediate withdrawal of all hostile forces, and the United Nations followed suit, with most of the British Commonwealth (made up of countries that are former British colonies) voting against the mother country. Britain, having no choice, pulled out. The Israelis, happy to have won another victory against Egypt, retreated back across the Sinai and went home.

Arab prisoners taken in the Suez war. Thoroughly defeated on the battlefield, Egypt won a diplomatic victory and retained control of the canal when world opinion forced the invading forces to withdraw.

UPI/BETTMANN NEWSPHOTOS

Prime Minister Anthony Eden of Britain is hung in effigy in Cairo following the invasion of Egypt in 1956. Britain's action aroused further hostility toward it among the Arab nations, while Nasser's aggressive stance made him a hero in the Arab world.

Although badly defeated in the field, Egypt had scored a moral victory in the court of world opinion and taken control of the canal. The military victors, Britain and France, were the diplomatic and economic losers.

Though the Egyptian military defeat had been no less thorough than the one suffered against Israel in 1947-48, Nasser emerged as the undisputed hero of the Arab world. His action in nationalizing the canal had exposed the British and French colonizers before the world as invaders and oppressors. Smiling Palestinian refugees carried pictures of Nasser in the back of their trucks as they returned to the Gaza Strip. Residents of Port Said cheered as the last British soldier departed. Egypt's defeat had been Nasser's triumph.

6

The Raïs

Before the Suez war — in June 1956 — he had been elected president of Egypt, but to Egypt's masses he was more than a mere political leader. They called him the *Raïs* (rah-EES), the Boss.

There was no doubt who was in charge in Egypt. The RCC had been dissolved upon Nasser's unopposed election to the presidency. The vote for the presidency had also approved the constitution Nasser had provided the country, which made him, in effect, a dictator with powers unmitigated by any constitutional checks and balances. There was only one political party, Nasser's National Union party, and no national legislature, although Nasser promised that elections for a legislature would be held at an unspecified date in the future.

Nasser strengthened his hold on power by maintaining a large internal security apparatus. Egyptians grew accustomed to having their mail read. Those with telephones had their lines tapped. The police kept track of possible opponents of the regime. Suspected disloyalty was punished by detention without trial. Detainees were often held in prison camps in the desert.

The Arab world and Arab policies possessed an irresistible attraction for [Nasser] and those fighting for independence or for changes of regime looked to him as their leader.
—DEREK HOPWOOD
British historian

Nasser at the opening of an oil refinery. After he reclaimed the Suez Canal, Nasser held absolute power in Egypt. There was only one political party, and opponents of the regime were often detained without trial.

After Suez, as far as most Egyptians were concerned, Nasser was Egypt. This extravagant admiration sometimes bordered on worship. "Gamal, O Lord," wrote Anwar Sadat in a children's book he authored, "is your magnificent creation, your conquering genius, your true servant."

Nasser had made Egypt the rising star of Arab nationalism. Egypt occupied a unique position within the Arab world. Indeed, there were some

In February 1958 Nasser and Syrian president Shukri al Kuwatly united their countries to form the United Arab Republic (U.A.R.). Nasser regarded the merger as the first step toward the eventual union of all the Arab nations.

Egyptians who argued that Egypt was not truly Arab at all but was an African or Mediterranean nation. Nasser disagreed, feeling that by virtue of its language, Arabic; religion, predominantly Islam; and heritage, Egypt was an Arab nation. Moreover, in his book *The Philosophy of the Revolution* Nasser argued that Egypt was to take a leadership position within the Arab, Muslim, and African worlds — the "three circles" within which Egypt existed.

I have an exact knowledge of the frontiers of the Arab nation . . . . These frontiers end where my propaganda no longer rouses an echo. Beyond this point, something else begins, a foreign world which does not concern me.
—NASSER

Nasser at Mecca, the city of Muhammad and the holy city of Islam. Each Muslim is required to make a pilgrimage to Mecca during his lifetime. Nasser believed that Egyptian leadership would unite the Arab, African, and Islamic worlds.

In his radio broadcasts, called the *Voice of the Arabs*, which had great influence within the Arab world, Nasser argued that a community of interests united the Arab nations. Such petty differences as the rivalry between the royal families of Saudi Arabia and Jordan and Iraq had to be put aside in favor of the elements that united the Arabs — their language, their religion, and most important, their common heritage as nations oppressed by the greed and arrogance of the West. United, the nations of the Arab world could stand up to Israel and the West.

A modest first step along the road to Arab consolidation, thought Nasser, would be union with another Arab country. Syria — fraught with disunity and political strife — seemed a likely candidate. Wedged between its enemy Israel to the south and the pro-Western countries of Turkey and Iraq to the north and east, Syria in the 1950s was caught in a tug-of-war. The Soviet Union and the United States vied for Syrian allegiance. While Syria had the Middle East's only powerful communist party, the *Baath* (Resurrection) party dominated. The Baaths opposed both the United States and the Soviet Union and sought Arab unity, self-determination, and independence. The Baath viewpoint held sway, and in early 1958 Syria proposed union with Egypt. Nasser accepted — with grave reservations. Syria appeared at times to be almost ungovernable, but this strange merger of geographically separated countries seemed to Nasser a necessary first step toward the goal of Arab unity.

Nasser addresses Syrian troops. The partnership between Egypt and Syria lasted only three years and was undermined by Syrian objections to the dominant and aggressive role Nasser played.

On February 21, 1958, 99.9 percent of Egyptian and Syrian voters ratified the articles of unification that created the United Arab Republic (U.A.R.). The new nation contained half of the population and a quarter of the land of the Arab Middle East, but it was fated not to last.

A number of problems plagued the U.A.R. from the beginning. Despite Nasser's calls for Arab unity, the Arab world was far from united. In his radio broadcasts, Nasser had bitterly denounced King Hussein of Jordan. His enmity toward Hussein had begun when he learned that the king had intended to sign the Baghdad Pact. Nasser's denunciations aroused popular support within Jordan against the king, making it impossible for Hussein to sign the pact. He continued to use his radio broadcasts against Hussein, inciting the Palestinians within

U.S. tanks landing in Beirut, Lebanon, in August 1958. Western nations felt that Nasser's message of Arab nationalism and opposition to Western interference in Arab affairs destabilized the region. The U.S. intervention in Lebanon was in response to Nasser's support for Muslim rebels opposing the government of Camille Chamoun.

Jordan against him, and also denounced Iraq, where Hussein's cousin Faisal was king. The two monarchs naturally distrusted Nasser. Others within the Arab world were also suspicious, believing that his call for one unified Arab nation was really a call for an Arab nation with Egypt, and Nasser, at its head. In February 1958 Jordan and Iraq merged their countries in the Arab Union. Arab distrust of Nasser was not eased by his denigrations of the Arab Union or his announced intention to unite the Arab nations "whether they like it or not." The divisiveness within the Arab world increased with the assassination of Faisal in July 1958 by Arab nationalists purportedly backed by the U.A.R.

Nasser and Prince Mohammed al-Badr of Yemen and other members of the Yemeni delegation in March 1958. Nasser sent Egyptian troops to support the republican revolutionaries who overthrew al-Badr shortly after he succeeded his father on the Yemeni throne in September 1961, embroiling Egypt in a prolonged civil war.

These problems were mirrored within the U.A.R. Egypt was not, as the terms of the unification stated, merely the southern province of the U.A.R. She was the dominant partner, and Syria was in effect an occupied country. Middle-class Syrians charged that Egypt got the better end of the economic deal; moreover, they did not care for the drift toward tighter economic controls that characterized Nasser's version of Arab socialism, toward which he was moving increasingly in the late 1950s. The

By the mid-1960s Cairo had become a center of the Arab and African worlds. The location of the headquarters of the Arab League there was indicative of the leading role Nasser had played in promoting Arab unity.

U.A.R. came to an end in September 1961 when the Syrian army seized power and declared Syria an independent country again. Nasser refused to use force to preserve the union. "Arabs should not kill Arabs," he said.

To the chagrin of Western and Middle Eastern leaders, Nasser continued to believe that his standing as the self-proclaimed champion of Arab nationalism gave him the right to intervene in matters where Arab interests were affected. His radio broad-

Peasants receive medical supplies provided by the UN. The social aspects of Nasser's revolution proved harder to implement than the political aspect. Exacerbated by continued widespread poverty, Egyptian health standards remained among the world's lowest, particularly in rural areas.

UPI/BETTMANN NEWSPHOTOS

casts urged Muslim rebels within Lebanon to revolt against the government of President Camille Chamoun. When rioting and demonstrations against the government broke out in May 1958, Lebanon filed a formal complaint with the UN alleging that the U.A.R. had intentionally interfered with its internal affairs. It was said that rebels were harbored and trained in Syria. The Soviet Union openly supported Nasser, while the United States flew arms to the beleaguered Lebanese government. By late June there was open fighting between government troops and the rebels. In July U.S. marines landed in Lebanon and a temporary peace ensued. Nasser vociferously condemned what he saw as another

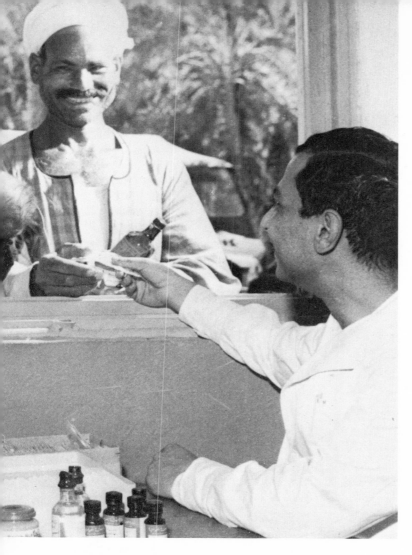

instance of high-handed Western intervention in Arab matters. The 10 Arab nations at the UN secured the passage of a resolution requesting the withdrawal of the U.S. troops and calling on each other to abstain from interfering in the internal affairs of their countries. New elections were held in Lebanon, and Chamoun was voted from office. One of the rebel leaders, Rashid Karami, was chosen as Lebanon's prime minister. The Lebanon crisis was seen in the Arab world as a triumph for Nasser, although the portion of the UN resolution regarding noninterference in internal affairs by Arab nations was viewed as being at least partly directed toward him.

Another, more overt and less successful, instance of Nasser's intervention into Arab affairs outside of Egypt occurred in the fall of 1962 when a rebellion overthrew the pro-Western monarchy in Yemen, a remote country on the southwestern coast of the Arabian Peninsula. Backed by Saudi Arabia, militant royalists rose up against the new regime, and Nasser sent 70,000 Egyptian soldiers to put down the counterrevolution. The civil war in Yemen lasted five years before a negotiated settlement was reached that allowed Nasser to recall his troops. Five years of fighting among Arabs did not ease the sus-

Though Nasser's health troubled him in the 1960s and he grew frustrated in his attempts to implement widespread social progress, he maintained a strong hold on power. To his countrymen he was synonymous with an independent Egypt. They called him the *Raïs* — the Boss.

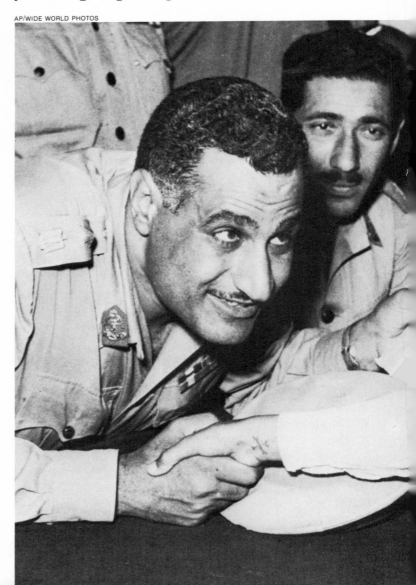

picions of those Arabs who felt that Nasser's rhetoric of a united Arab world really meant an Arab world under Egyptian domination.

Besides the elusive goal of pan-Arabism, Nasser had also dreamed of a united Africa with Cairo as its capital. This, too, proved to be sheer fantasy. His vision of a united Islamic world was no less fantastic, for most of the world's Muslims are not Arabs.

While Nasser sought to export his message to the other Arab nations, his revolution had been less than completely successful at home. After the first wave of revolutionary reforms in agricultural land-

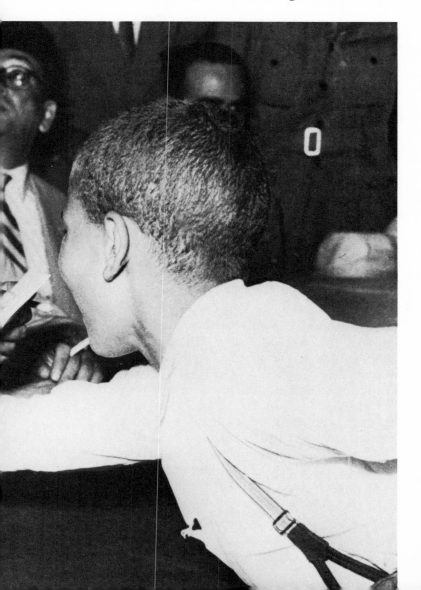

The ancient temple of Ramses III, a legacy of Egypt's historic past, had to be relocated to make way for the Aswan dam, symbol of Nasser's modernization of his country.

ownership, the pace of social reform had been slow. Influenced by the friendship of the Soviet Union and his repeated exposure to the communist economy of Yugoslavia, with which he was very impressed, Nasser moved the Egyptian economy towards state socialism, whereby most of the leading industries and corporations were owned by the state. (By contrast, under communism, as in the Soviet Union, industries are theoretically owned collectively by the workers; under capitalism they are privately or individually owned.) In 1961 there began a series of arrests of so-called reactionary capitalists, followed by the confiscation of their property. As many as 500 wealthy families had their assets expropriated. Many banks, insurance companies, and other corporations were placed under government control. The government also took over most of the newspapers. In 1962 Egypt was officially declared a socialist state. Nasser claimed that socialism had been imposed on Egypt by "historical inevitability," not by any ideological predisposition on his part.

Nasser's was an Egyptian brand of socialism, termed by him "Arab socialism." Unlike the hardline Soviet ideology, which discouraged the practice of religion, Arab socialism placed no restrictions on religious worship. Indeed, Nasser viewed Islam as an integral part of the Egyptian identity. At least half the economy remained in the private sector even though 80 percent of Egyptian industry was owned by the state. There was a reason. Egypt remained a predominantly agricultural nation. Industrialization, undertaken with help from the Soviet Union, had not made much headway. The Aswan project was completed by 1970, but the huge dam, while useful, became a giant symbol of Egypt's essentially agrarian economy, still dependent on the waters of the Nile.

Reforming Egypt had proven harder than Nasser expected. Many of the same problems remained. The army remained weak, as evidenced by the events of the Suez crisis and the inability to achieve a victory in Yemen. The economic inequities of the nation had proved difficult to redress, and the imposition of a state-planned economy required a large number of bureaucrats to administer it, reminiscent to many Egyptians of the bureaucracy that had administered the nation during its years of foreign domination. The "healthy democracy" the Free Officers had wanted to foster had been long forgotten — there were no opposition parties. There was only Nasser, surrounded by his close aides.

The long years of hard work had wearied him. His health had begun to fail. Diabetes, first diagnosed in the late 1950s, led to a heart condition. He grew suspicious, distrustful, and increasingly intro-

The Aswan dam was completed in 1970. Its construction was made possible by funding and engineers from the Soviet Union, to which Nasser turned for assistance after being rejected by the United States.

Lights in the Cairo Hilton hotel spell out the name "Nasser" during a celebration in June 1964. Despite his inability to solve the country's economic problems, Egyptians continued to revere Nasser as the architect of their independence and champion of Arab interests.

verted. Periods of depression assailed him, and he began shutting himself away in Alexandria for long months at a time. He broke off consultations with associates who were outspoken, preferring to surround himself with yes-men, among whom Anwar Sadat was the most obsequious. "If he would occasionally vary his way of expressing agreement instead of forever saying 'Yes, sir!'," Nasser once remarked, "that would be easier on my nerves."

The most pressing problem in the Arab world, and the one most likely to unite the often quarreling Arab nations, remained Israel and the plight of the

Palestinians. Since the 1957 truce ending the Suez crisis, Egypt and Israel had existed in a kind of limbo, technically at war but actually in a state of de facto peace, broken by Egyptian and Palestinian guerrilla attacks on Israel and Israeli retaliations. In the early 1960s Nasser faced increased criticism from an Arab world that looked to him to take aggressive action in solving the Israel question. While Egypt insisted that it would not fight a war with Israel until the Arab states were unified, Israel readied itself for what it regarded as an inevitable war.

7

The Last Pharaoh

Palestinian guerrillas had been harassing Israel ever since the end of the 1948 Palestine war, operating from bases in Syria, Jordan, and Gaza. The 1960s saw an increase in this activity, as the Palestinians grew increasingly restive with their exile. While many Arab nations paid lip service allegiance to the Palestinian cause, the leftist government that came to power in Syria in 1966 offered active support to the Palestinian guerrillas, which increased their activities against Israel. Each attack was answered by Israeli retaliation, sometimes retaliation far in excess of the severity of the attacks and often not directly aimed at the attackers. Under increased criticism in the Arab world for his "torpor" in spearheading the Arab opposition to Israel, Nasser was induced in early November 1966 to pledge support to Syria should the nation come under Israeli attack. On November 13, 1966, three Israeli soldiers were killed at the Syrian border. Reluctant to challenge Syria and Egypt, Israel launched a raid on the Jordanian town of Samu, leaving 18 dead and 134 wounded. Tensions escalated. In early 1967 border clashes led to dogfights between Israeli and Syrian aircraft over Damascus, the Syrian capital. Each new incident threatened to result in full-scale war.

I have given the Egyptian people dignity.
—NASSER

Nasser delivers a speech at a session of the Palestine National Assembly in Cairo in 1965. Although during the 1960s he put aside the issue of Israel to concentrate on domestic matters, the Palestinians and the other Arab nations looked to Nasser to take a strong stance against the Israelis.

UPI/BETTMANN NEWSPHOTOS

UN peacekeeping forces had been stationed in the Gaza Strip, a thin piece of land along the Mediterranean between Israel and Egypt, since the Suez crisis of 1956. When Nasser asked the UN forces to withdraw in May 1967, Israel interpreted it as a harbinger of war.

The world press reported that both the Israelis and the Syrians were planning to attack. Reports supplied to Nasser by Soviet intelligence said that an Israeli attack on Syria was imminent. While Nasser would later claim that he was not bound and determined on war with Israel at this point, his obligations to Syria led him to take steps that were perceived by Israel as threatening. On May 15 he put Egyptian military forces on alert and sent troops into the Sinai. He also sent word to the commander of the UN peacekeeping force in the Sinai, which had been in place since the cessation of the Suez hostilities, requesting that all UN troops withdraw immediately so that Egypt might act against Israel "should an act of aggression be committed."

To the Israelis this amounted to an announcement that Egypt was about to attack. If so, Israel had been well prepared for years. The Israeli military had been planning since 1957 for the next round of the conflict.

The next move centered on the Gulf of Aqaba, a thin finger of water dividing the Arabian Peninsula from the Sinai Peninsula at the northern end of the Red Sea.

Egyptian troops took over a small port city on Tiran Island in the Strait of Tiran, through which ships must pass to enter the gulf. Cairo then announced that the gulf would be closed to Israeli shipping, thereby blocking access to the port city of Eilat in southern Israel. Much of Israel's oil supply came through the Gulf of Aqaba from Iran. The closing of the Gulf of Aqaba was greeted with enthusiastic applause throughout the Arab world. Nasser was again a hero, but not for long.

Israel struck first, and the blow was devastating. In a precisely timed, well-coordinated attack on the morning of June 5, Israeli planes bombed Egyptian airfields and wiped out Nasser's air force. Out of some 340 operational aircraft — fighters, bombers, transports, and trainers — 300 were left in burning heaps on the ground. The attacks were so sudden most of the Egyptian pilots were at breakfast or still asleep when the Israelis struck. More Israeli raids quickly destroyed the much smaller Syrian and Jordanian air forces. (Jordan had signed a mutual defense agreement with Egypt on May 30.)

Nasser (center) views Egyptian military maneuvers. Egypt's military weakness was revealed once again by its shattering defeat by Israel in the Six-Day War of 1967.

Tired of Nasser's provocative actions, Israel launched the Six-Day War with air raids that destroyed virtually all of Egypt's air force. When Egyptian artillery bombardments and guerrilla harassment continued after the cease-fire, an Israeli bombing mission destroyed the oil refinery at Port Suez. Without an air force, Egypt was powerless to prevent such raids.

With absolute mastery of the skies assured, Israeli ground forces rolled over everything in their path, all the way across the Sinai Peninsula to the Suez Canal. By June 11 the Six-Day War was history. Israel had defeated three Arab armies and captured much Arab territory. In addition to the Sinai, Israeli forces had overrun the Arab part of Jerusalem, the West Bank of the Jordan River, and the strategic Golan Heights along the Syrian border.

The Arab losses were staggering. Some 20,000 Egyptian soldiers were wounded or killed. Hundreds of tanks and trucks, thousands upon thousands of weapons, piles of equipment and material, were left behind in the desert sand.

The loss almost killed Nasser. Sadat claimed he looked like a corpse — gray and lifeless — for months afterward. In the immediate aftermath of the defeat, Nasser appeared on television and announced his resignation. The long story had come to an end; Nasser was finished.

His people would not let him go. They took to the streets, shouting his name, pleading with him to stay. The National Assembly — Nasser's rubber-stamp parliament — voted unanimously to request that the Raïs remain in office until all Egyptian territory was liberated.

There were more losses to ponder. The Suez Canal was now no more than a fortified line between two armies, closed to shipping, its millions of dollars in revenue gone. The Sinai oil fields, which supplied most of Egypt's petroleum, were in enemy hands. Thousands of refugees poured from the war zone into Cairo and other overpopulated areas.

If Nasser was not to blame for the debacle, then it stood to reason that someone was responsible. Nasser could not bring himself to blame anyone else, but to his dismay he discovered that his former army chief of staff was plotting against him. Dozens of high government officials and military leaders were subsequently arrested and charged with treason. Some of Nasser's oldest friends and associates were included in the indictments. For Nasser this was the bitterest pill of all.

Israeli soldiers heading toward the front pass a truckload of Egyptian prisoners. Egypt lost more than 20,000 men and most of its military resources during the Six-Day War, which ranks as one of the most serious military disasters in Middle Eastern history.

A Soviet-made tank and shells captured by Israel from Egypt during the Six-Day War. The overwhelming defeat greatly damaged Nasser's prestige; his health suffered and he attempted to resign from office.

He turned to the Soviet Union for help. Egypt needed planes, guns, supplies, and, most of all, technological aid — the army needed advisers to teach undereducated Egyptian soldiers how to handle modern weaponry. The Soviet Union was willing to send all the defensive weapons Nasser wanted, especially anti-aircraft missiles. The Soviet Union also agreed to supply technicians, and over the next few years Soviet military personnel became a common sight in Egypt.

Late in 1967 Arab leaders met at a summit conference in Khartoum, the capital of the Sudan. The parley was an embarrassment for Nasser, for he had to face the conservative, pro-Western Arab leaders he had so often denounced and ask them for charity. Saudi Arabia demanded that Nasser negotiate an end to the war in Yemen, which he was only too glad to do. In return for this, the Saudis, along with other oil-rich kingdoms, agreed to compensate Egypt for her war losses until such time as she regained her captured territory and lost revenues.

There appeared to be little hope of that occurring in the near future. Despite diplomatic pressure from her staunchest ally, the United States, Israel showed no willingness to retreat to its prewar borders. Nasser knew that Egypt could not undertake another war in the forseeable future. Worse, clashes between Egyptian and Israeli forces continued, with Egypt suffering the worst of it. Israeli pilots flew American Phantom jets to raid factories in the suburbs of Cairo. Egypt was unable to put a plane in the air to defend its cities.

Worst of all, Egypt was now dependent on another foreign power — the Soviet Union. Nasser was grateful for Soviet aid but was suspicious of the Soviets, and he was determined to resist any attempt to influence his policymaking.

Nasser's foreign policy reversed itself by 1969, as Nasser decided to seek U.S. mediation of a settlement with Israel. In 1970 his acceptance of U.S. terms for a cease-fire along the Suez, where skirmishes with the Israelis continued, outraged anti-Western Arab states such as Syria, who feared that Egypt would seek a negotiated peace with Israel.

Nasser viewing a Soviet troop formation in Moscow. Desperate for financial, military, and technological aid in the aftermath of the Six-Day War, Nasser turned to the Soviets for help.

Sandbags and a soldier in the streets of Cairo in 1969 serve as reminders that Egypt had been officially at war with Israel since 1948. Nasser's acceptance of a cease-fire with Israel in 1970 was bitterly opposed by other Arab states and the Palestinians.

(The nations of the Arab League, of which Egypt was a member, had been officially at war with Israel since that nation's independence. Although various cease-fires had been negotiated, the Arab League remained unalterably opposed to peace with Israel.)

The Palestinians regarded negotiations with Israel as a betrayal. Wary of depending on the support of the Arab nations in regaining their homeland, under the leadership of the Palestine Liberation Organization (PLO) they escalated their terrorist campaign, hoping to attract worldwide attention to their cause and sabotage any negotiated peace.

Though Nasser remained firmly in power in Egypt, the defeat by Israel and his apparent willingness to negotiate compromised him in the eyes of the more militant Arabs. This was especially grating to him because, as he saw it, he had led the way to militant Arab nationalism.

Meanwhile his health continued to worsen. He lacked strength and had frequent chest pains. In September 1969 he had a mild heart attack but recovered sufficiently to go back to his duties. His aides begged him to lighten his work load. "Egypt needs me on a daily basis," he answered. "How can I refuse her?"

It was not only Egypt that needed him. Arab unity faced a new threat in September 1970. The PLO (many of the Palestinians lived within Jordan) and the army of Jordan's King Hussein were engaged in a bloody civil war that had been provoked by extremist elements within the Palestinian movement. Hussein feared the growing strength of the PLO and claimed that it sought to dethrone him. The Jordanian army attacked PLO strongholds and refugee camps in Jordan. The fighting resulted in appalling casualties, mostly on the Palestinian side.

Nasser with Sadat (center) and Yasir Arafat in September 1970. Nasser mediated a cease-fire between the PLO and Jordan's King Hussein, who had been fighting a civil war within Jordan. It was his last major achievement.

AP/WIDE WORLD PHOTOS

A rare photo of Nasser with his wife and five children. Nasser died of a heart attack in September 1970, immediately following the conference at which he reconciled Arafat and Hussein.

Nasser called an urgent meeting in Cairo of Arab heads of state. Tempers flared, but Nasser's quiet diplomacy won the day. Even Nasser's severest critics admitted that the conference was among his finest hours. He was the soul of moderation, gently urging both sides to settle their differences peacefully. Above all, he pleaded that the fighting in Jordan be stopped immediately.

The conference was adjourned on September 28, 1970. The results were impressive. Hussein and the PLO leader, Yasir Arafat, signed a cease-fire agreement. A photograph made the rounds in the Arab press, showing Hussein and Arafat smiling and shaking hands. They had been mortal enemies the day before. Nasser the peacemaker stood behind them, a tired but satisfied look on his face.

It was to be Nasser's last achievement. On his way back from the airport, where he had seen the last of the delegates off, he suffered a severe heart attack. By six o'clock that evening, Gamal Abdel Nasser was dead.

Anwar Sadat, whom Nasser had appointed sole vice-president in 1969, succeeded him. Under Sadat the military was rebuilt, and Egypt fought Israel again in the 1973 Yom Kippur War. Expanded negotiations with the Israelis resulted, along with the return of some of the occupied territory. In 1979 a peace treaty between Egypt and Israel was signed.

But all this was still in Egypt's future at the time of Nasser's death. Egypt had always had a past, but it was Nasser who had given her a future.

The independent nation of Egypt had lost her firstborn son. Crowds of weeping mourners surrounded the funeral procession. Hands reached out for one last touch; tears flowed. "Gamal, you will live forever!" they shouted, the words choking in their throats.

It cannot be said that the Nasser regime was an unqualified success. Years of neglect, misrule, and colonial exploitation left Egypt with deep-seated economic woes that proved resistant to Nasser's ministrations. His dream of building the Egyptian military into a capable fighting force was never achieved, a failure attested to by Egypt's defeats by Israel. He maintained power by using secret police, domestic surveillance, and clamping down on all opposition, not through the exercise of true democratic institutions. The democracy the Free Officers promised was never developed.

Yet Nasser restored Egypt's pride. For the first time in centuries Egypt had an Egyptian as leader, someone who spoke for their own interests, not

Lebanese citizens in Beirut mourn the death of Nasser. The man who had freed Egypt from foreign domination and championed Arab unity and independence was mourned throughout the Arab world.

those of a foreign power. His intransigent opposition to British and Western domination of Egypt and the Arab world fired the imaginations of both Egyptians and Arabs. To Egyptians he was the architect of their nation's independence; to other Arabs he was the voice of Arab nationalism, urging them to take pride in their heritage and join together to promote Arab interests. His nationalization of the Suez Canal and refusal to bow to the resulting pressure from the West, in the form of the invasion by Britain, France, and Israel, illustrated that it was possible for Arabs to act independently to achieve their own goals, not simply at the behest of their colonial masters. The militant Arab nationalism that has been at the forefront of Middle Eastern politics since the 1950s stands as his historic legacy.

In a tomb on the outskirts of Cairo, they laid him to rest. His failures were forgotten. His people would only remember that before he ruled them, Egypt had been in bondage. Now it was free.

> *No wonder we clung to our leader after the defeat and that we made his personal existence a substitute for victory or a synonym for it, because he made us feel by all available means that there existed in Egypt and the whole Arab world only one intelligence, one power, one personality.*
> —TAWFIG AL-HAKIN
> Egyptian author

Further Reading

Aufderheide, Patricia. *Sadat.* New York: Chelsea House, 1985.

Hasou, Tawfig Y. *The Struggle for the Arab World.* London: KPI, 1985.

Hopwood, Derek. *Egypt: Politics and Society 1945–1981.* London: Allen & Unwin, 1982.

Joesten, Joachim. *Nasser: The Rise to Power.* Westport, CT: Greenwood Press, 1960.

Lacouture, Jean. *Nasser: A Biography.* New York: Knopf, 1973.

Nasser, Gamal Abdel. *Egypt's Liberation: The Philosophy of the Revolution.* Washington, DC: Public Affairs Press, 1955.

Nutting, Anthony. *Nasser.* New York: Dutton, 1972.

Vatikiotis, P. J. *Nasser and His Generation.* New York: St. Martin's Press, 1978.

Chronology

Jan. 15, 1918	Born Gamal Abdel Nasser in Alexandria
1921	Nasser family moves to village of Beni-Mor
1925	Nasser moves to Cairo
1935	Sir Samuel Hoare reiterates British position on Egyptian colonial status; students protest in Cairo; Nasser organizes a march on a British garrison; King Fuad restores constitutional rights and calls for national elections
1936	Wafdist government of Nahas Pasha arranges for evacuation of Egypt by British; British maintain military presence in Suez Canal Zone
March 17, 1937	Nasser enters the Royal Military Academy at Abbassia
July 1, 1938	Graduates from academy; assigned to infantry post in Mankabad
Feb. 4, 1942	British use the military to pressure King Fuad into accepting an anti-Nazi cabinet
Oct. 19, 1942	British forces defeat German *Afrika Korps* at El Alamein
1946	Nasser admitted to Army Staff College
1947	The United Nations officially partitions Palestine; Israelis and Palestinians clash
1948	Nasser graduates from Army Staff College; Israeli state is founded
Jan. 26, 1952	Riots in Cairo in reaction to British attack on an Egyptian police barracks in the Canal Zone
July 23, 1952	Nasser leads the revolt of the Free Officers
June 1956	Elected president of Republic of Egypt
July 1956	Nationalizes the Suez Canal
Oct. 29, 1956	Israeli army invades the Sinai
Nov. 6, 1956	Cease-fire in the Suez
1958	Egypt and Syria form the United Arab Republic (U.A.R.)
1961	Syria withdraws from U.A.R.
1963	Nasser commits Egyptian troops to support the republic of Yemen in civil war
June 1967	Egypt suffers major defeat in Six-Day War with Israel
Sept. 1970	Nasser forges agreement between King Hussein of Jordan and Yasir Arafat of the Palestine Liberation Organization (PLO)
July 1970	Accepts U.S. plan for political settlement with Israel
Sept. 28, 1970	Gamal Abdel Nasser dies of a heart attack in Cairo

Index

John DeChancie is a writer who lives and works in western Pennsylvania. Active for a time in motion picture and television production, he eventually turned to full-time writing, publishing his first novel in 1983. Since then he has written nonfiction and several science fiction and fantasy novels. He is married and has two children.

Arthur M. Schlesinger, jr., taught history at Harvard for many years and is currently Albert Schweitzer Professor of the Humanities at City University of New York. He is the author of numerous highly praised works in American history and has twice been awarded the Pulitzer Prize. He served in the White House as special assistant to Presidents Kennedy and Johnson.

92
Nas

DeChancie, John

Gamal Abdel Nasser

DATE DUE

NOV 3 '84			

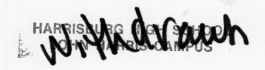